Pamela P. Peterson, CFA
Florida State University
David R. Peterson
Florida State University

Company Performance and Measures of Value Added

The Research Foundation of
The Institute of Chartered Financial Analysts

Research Foundation Publications

Company Performance and Measures of Value Added

This publication is designed to provide accurate and authoritative information in regard to the subject matter covered. It is sold with the understanding that the publisher is not engaged in rendering legal, accounting, or other professional service. If legal advice or other expert assistance is required, the services of a competent professional should be sought.

ISBN 0-943205-36-0

Printed in the United States of America

December 1996

Editorial Staff

Maryann Dupes
Editor

Jaynee M. Dudley
Manager, Educational Products

Marsha Gainey
Assistant Editor

Diane B. Hamshar
Typesetting/Layout

Mission

The Research Foundation's mission is to identify, fund, and publish research that is relevant to the AIMR Global Body of Knowledge and useful for AIMR member investment practitioners and investors.

The Research Foundation of
The Institute of Chartered Financial Analysts
P.O. Box 3668
Charlottesville, Virginia 22903
U.S.A.
Telephone: 804-980-3655
Fax: 804-980-3634
E-mail: rf@aimr.org
World Wide Web: http://www.aimr.org/aimr/research/research.html

Biographies of Authors

Pamela P. Peterson, CFA, is a professor of finance at Florida State University, where she teaches undergraduate courses in corporate finance and doctoral courses in empirical research methods. She is also an associate editor for various financial publications. She has been a CFA Review Program instructor in Raleigh, North Carolina; Salt Lake City, Utah; and Zurich, Switzerland. Professor Peterson has published more than 25 articles in various academic journals and is the author of *Financial Management and Analysis*, published by McGraw-Hill. Prior to working at Florida State University, Professor Peterson was at Arthur Andersen & Company. Her research interests are capital structure issues, analysts' forecasts, and empirical methods. Professor Peterson received a B.S. degree from Miami University (Ohio) in accountancy and a Ph.D. from the University of North Carolina at Chapel Hill in finance.

David R. Peterson is a professor of finance at Florida State University, where he teaches undergraduate and doctoral courses in investments and valuation theory. Professor Peterson has published more than 45 articles in various academic journals. He served as an *ad hoc* reviewer for the National Science Foundation and for various financial publications. Before coming to Florida State University, Professor Peterson taught at Duke University and the University of North Carolina at Chapel Hill and worked at J.P. Baldwin Company and Continental Illinois National Bank. His research interests are capital market securities, analysts' forecasts, and market efficiency. Professor Peterson holds a B.S. from Miami University (Ohio) in economics and a Ph.D. from the University of North Carolina at Chapel Hill in finance.

Contents

Foreword

Few skills are more essential to a security analyst than the ability to evaluate a company's performance in a concise and compelling manner. Given the importance that firm valuation plays in financial markets, the wealth of research literature on the topic (including contributions from such giants in the investment management profession as Gordon, Graham, Dodd, Modigliani, Miller, and Tobin) is not surprising. In spite of all the intellectual firepower that has been aimed at the issue, however, performance evaluation can hardly be considered a permanently solved puzzle. Indeed, recent years have witnessed the ascent of a sometimes confusing array of terms—EVA®, MVA™, CFROI—representing state-of-the-art statistical measures intended to take the place in analysts' hearts and minds of the traditional market-based metrics, such as return on assets (ROA) and return on equity (ROE).[1] Although it is widely acknowledged that these new methods are often useful, it is not clearly understood where they fit in the analyst's toolkit.

In this tutorial, Pamela Peterson and David Peterson help make sense of these contemporary developments and provide a context in which to compare the new with the old. The authors also do a great job of dispelling some current myths about the latest generation of evaluation techniques. For example, one interesting aspect of these new performance tools is that they are not all that new. Economic value added has its origins in the notion of economic profit, first advanced a century ago; cash flow return on investment is an adaptation of the well-established internal rate of return. The authors' impartial insights prove particularly valuable to the reader in that much of what is presently known about EVA and CFROI comes from the consulting firms that promote these statistics.

Peterson and Peterson begin their analysis with a summary of conventional measures of company performance, such as the myriad return ratios (e.g., earnings power, ROA, ROE), book-to-market value, and Tobin's q. Against this backdrop, they then develop the intuition for the so-called value-added measures, including the aforementioned EVA—along with its companion measure, market value added—and CFROI. These explanations are at once user friendly and illuminating; in fact, the careful pedagogy contained in this section is arguably the most valuable part of the tutorial. Taking the case of Hershey Foods Corporation, the authors show how these measures can be constructed from publicly available accounting data using each of several different methods. Along the way, they highlight the many assumptions that the analyst must make to apply these approaches in practice. I suspect that this section will serve both industry and academia as a "how to" manual in this area for years to come.

The authors conclude their study with an empirical analysis of how closely the value-added measures are linked to stock returns, which they suggest is the ultimate test of a company's performance. In particular, they calculate the extent to which both the market-based and value-added metrics correlate with various return calculations. Peterson and Peterson start from the position that because "value-added measures are theoretically more closely related to firm value than the simpler traditional measures," they should also be more closely related empirically. In this regard, their results are somewhat surprising. Although stock returns are, in fact, highly correlated

---

[1] EVA and MVA are trademarks of Stern, Stewart & Company.

©The Research Foundation of the ICFA

with both the conventional and value-added statistics, the advantage that the latter holds over the former is slight. Furthermore, the authors document some important biases of the EVA and MVA measures involving the market capitalizations of the firms in their sample.

Although the authors express disappointment in these empirical findings, the reader certainly should not be disappointed. To the contrary, this research performs two important services. First, and quite possibly foremost, it provides a thoughtful primer on how to translate "value-added" theory into practice. Second, it offers an unbiased and critical examination of the advantage of these tools. Although the authors' analysis supports the usefulness of the modern measures, they point out the fact that nontrivial costs are involved in the application. The material in this tutorial is at the heart of what a security analyst needs to know to perform his or her job in today's market, and the Research Foundation is pleased to have been part of its development.

Keith C. Brown, CFA
Research Director
The Research Foundation of the
Institute of Chartered Financial Analysts

Acknowledgments

We would like to thank Keith Brown, CFA, for helpful direction and comments; Sam Eddins and Bartley Madden of HOLT Value Associates, Rawley Thomas of BCG/HOLT, and Lee Glasner for answering questions and supplying information concerning CFROI; and Al Ehrbar of Stern, Stewart & Company for answering questions regarding the economic-value-added approach. We would also like to thank the Research Foundation of the Institute of Chartered Financial Analysts, AIMR, and Florida State University for their support.

Pamela P. Peterson, CFA
David R. Peterson

1. Introduction

A business that operates in such a way as to maximize its owners' wealth allocates its own resources efficiently, which results in an efficient allocation of resources for society as a whole. Owners, employees, customers, and anyone else who has a stake in the business enterprise are all better off when its managers make decisions that maximize the value of the firm. Therefore, evaluating a firm's management on the basis of whether it maximizes the owners' wealth is a reasonable approach.

Evaluating a firm's performance seems to be a rather straightforward issue, but it is not. By focusing on the maximization of a stock's price, one might conclude that the higher the stock's price, the better the performance of the firm's management. But should management be penalized if the market declines? Should management be praised simply because the economy has recovered? Should management be rewarded for taking on excessive risks?

Evaluating a firm's performance is much more challenging than looking at its stock price, and evaluating the performance of specific managers is even more challenging. Regulators and shareholder activists have long complained about the way firms pay executives, especially when pay is not linked to performance. Even when executive pay is linked to performance, the issue of how to measure performance remains. If pay is linked to accounting earnings, the possibility exists that these accounting earnings can be manipulated to produce high pay for the executives at the expense of shareholders.[1] In recent years, executive compensation has been overhauled to improve the link between pay and performance by shifting pay packages to include stock options. Yet in many companies, such a link does not exist, and in others, the link is imperfect.[2]

Because of the need for better methods of evaluating performance, several consulting firms have been advocating performance evaluation methods that look at a firm's performance as a whole and the performance of specific managers. These methods are, in some cases, supplanting traditional methods of measuring performance, such as return on assets.

The purpose of this tutorial is to examine traditional and recently developed methods of evaluating firm performance. Our focus is on the performance of the firm as a whole, and we do not address the application of these measures to specific managers or products. But what we learn from applying these methods to firms as a whole may affect the application of these methods to specific managers.

How Value Is Created
A firm's management creates value when it makes decisions that provide benefits exceeding costs. These benefits may be received in the near or distant future, and the costs include the direct cost of the investment and a less obvious cost, the cost of capital.

---

[1]See, for example, the evidence produced in Healy (1985) and Holthausen, Larcker, and Sloan (1995).

[2]The link between pay and performance is highlighted in the *Business Week* special report by Byrne and Bongiorno (1995).

This benefit–cost analysis is the heart of the traditional capital-budgeting analysis. One common technique for analyzing these benefits and costs is the net present value method, which discounts uncertain future cash flows at some rate that reflects the cost of capital used in the investment. This cost of capital reflects the marginal cost of raising additional capital. The cost also reflects the risk inherent in the project; the greater the investment's risk, the greater its cost of capital.[3] The difference between the present value of these uncertain cash flows and the cost of the project (i.e., the investment outlay) is referred to as the project's net present value.

The net present value is expressed in terms of dollars of value. If the net present value is positive, the investment is expected to add value to the firm; if the net present value is negative, the investment is expected to reduce the value of the firm. Hence, the net present value is a measure of value added (if positive) or value subtracted (if negative).

Another often-used technique is the internal rate of return (IRR). In this approach to evaluating investment projects, the discount rate is determined (through iteration) so that it equates the future cash flows with the investment's explicit costs (i.e., the investment outlay). Stated equivalently, the IRR is the discount rate that equates the net present value to zero.

Use of the IRR requires first calculating the IRR (the project's "internal rate") and then comparing this rate with a rate that reflects the cost of capital. Once again, this cost of capital reflects the costs of the various sources of funds and the uncertainty associated with the investment. If the project's IRR exceeds this cost of capital (sometimes referred to as the "hurdle rate"), the project is value enhancing. If, on the other hand, the project's IRR is less than the cost of capital, the project is value reducing.

No matter the particular capital-budgeting technique used, the principles are the same: A firm should invest only in projects that enhance the value of the firm. So, where do these value-enhancing projects come from? In a competitive market in which many firms compete for available investment opportunities, value-enhancing projects should not exist. In other words, the cost of a project should be bid upward through competition so that no net benefit results from investing in the project. This explanation is rather gloomy and ignores the true source of value-enhancing projects—a firm's comparative or competitive advantage. Only through some advantage vis-à-vis its competitors can a firm invest in projects that enhance value.

A *comparative advantage* is the advantage one firm has over others in terms of the cost of producing or distributing goods or services. Wal-Mart Stores developed a comparative advantage over its competitors (such as Kmart Corporation) through its network of warehouses and its distribution system. Wal-Mart invested in a system of regional warehouses and in its own trucking system. By using the regional warehouse system instead of a national warehouse system or no warehouse system at all, Wal-Mart reduces its need for inventory. Furthermore, by having its own truck fleet, Wal-Mart is able to replenish store inventories more frequently than its competitors. Combined with bulk purchases and a unique customer approach (such as its "greeters"), Wal-Mart's comparative advantage in its warehousing and distribution systems has helped it grow to be a major, and very profitable, retailer in a short span of time.

A *competitive advantage* is the advantage one firm has over another because of the structure of the markets (input and output markets) in which they both operate. For example, one firm may have a competitive advantage because of barriers that prevent

---

[3]The key elements of the cost of capital concept in capital budgeting are that (1) the cost is a marginal cost (the cost on the next dollar of capital) and (2) the cost reflects the risk of the individual project. For a more detailed presentation of the cost of capital, see Appendix A.

other firms from entering the same market. Barriers to entering a market arise in the case of governmental regulations that limit the number of firms in a market, as with banks, or in the case of monopolies granted by the government, as in the past with local cable companies. A firm itself may create barriers to entry (with the help of the government) with patents and trademarks.

In cases in which no impediments to investment exist (that is, the market for investments is competitive), only through having some type of advantage can a firm make an investment and get more than the present value of the initial outlay back in return. The same basic principles applied here to individual projects can be applied when looking at the entire firm. If the firm's investments provide future benefits greater than their costs, the investments enhance the value of the firm. If the firm's investments provide future benefits that are less than their costs, this situation is detrimental to the value of the firm.

The idea of producing current value from future investment opportunities is reflected in the concept of franchise value, which is discussed by Kogelman and Leibowitz (1995) in their decomposition of the price-to-earnings ratio (P/E) into a franchise P/E and a base P/E.[4] In their analysis, future investment opportunities in excess of market returns are reflected in above-market P/Es.

From the perspective of analysts, the focus of performance evaluation is on the firm as a whole, not on individual investment decisions within the firm. The key to evaluating a firm's performance is, therefore, determining whether the firm's investment decisions as a whole are producing value for the shareholders. But no obvious technique exists for determining whether a firm's decisions produce value for shareholders because (1) no one has the ability to perfectly forecast future cash flows from investments, (2) no one has accurate measures of the risks of each investment, and (3) no one knows the precise cost of capital. Therefore, proxies must be used (however imperfect) to assess a firm's performance.

Relating New Performance Methods to Capital-Budgeting Techniques

The most prominent value-added techniques recently developed for evaluating a firm's performance are economic value added and market value added.[5,6] EVA and MVA measures have links to the fundamental valuation techniques and are based on the same valuation principles as the net present value capital-budgeting technique.

The net present value for a specific investment project is the estimate of change in the value of equity if the firm invests in the project. The value-added measures also produce an estimate of the change in the value of the firm, but they relate to the firm as a whole rather than a specific project. Furthermore, although net present value is forward looking (assisting management in making decisions dealing with the use of capital in the future), measuring a firm's performance using value-added techniques to help gauge how well management performed focuses on the decisions that have been made during a period

---

[4]This article is a continuation of their work in Leibowitz and Kogelman (1990); see also Leibowitz and Kogelman (1994).

[5]A detailed description of the value-added methods can be found in Stewart (1991).

[6]Another prominent valuation approach is the discounted cash flow approach advocated by McKinsey & Company and discussed by Copeland, Koller, and Murrin (1994, p. 116). This approach involves forecasting future periods' free cash flows, forecasting a firm's continuing value at the end of the forecast period, and discounting the future free cash flows and the continuing value at the firm's weighted-average cost of capital. Because this approach involves valuation based on forecasts, it is not a suitable device for evaluating performance, although it is useful in setting performance targets.

and the cost of capital that supported those investment decisions .

Economic value added is another name for the firm's economic profit. To estimate economic profit, the following key elements are necessary:

- calculation of the firm's operating profit from financial statement data, making adjustments to accounting profit to reflect a firm's results for a certain period;
- calculation of the cost of capital; and
- comparison of operating profit with the cost of capital.

The difference between the operating profit and the cost of capital is the estimate of the firm's economic profit, or economic value added.

A related measure, market value added, focuses on the market value of capital, as compared with the cost of capital. The following are key elements of market value added:

- calculation of the market value of capital;
- calculation of the capital invested; and
- comparison of the market value of capital with the capital invested.

The difference between the market value of capital and the amount of capital invested is the market value added. The primary distinction between economic value added and market value added is that the latter incorporates market data in the calculation.

An important part of performance evaluation is considering the controllable versus uncontrollable aspects of an investment. Consider the example of a good manager and a bad scenario. A manager of a firm may decide to invest in a risky project that is expected to produce cash flows sufficient to make up for the expected cost of capital. Some risk exists that the project may not be profitable, although this scenario is unlikely (i.e., a small chance exists that the project will be unprofitable), but no matter how slight this unprofitable scenario, this project is risky. After investing in the project, the unlikely scenario may in fact materialize and cause the investment decision to be value decreasing when, in fact, it was anticipated to be a profitable decision—assuming for the sake of this example that the manager made the correct investment decision (he or she was not omniscient). How should this manager's performance be evaluated? In a capital-budgeting sense, the manager made the correct decision. The tough part is figuring out how to evaluate the decision maker because an evaluation *after the fact* should hold the decision maker accountable for only those factors over which he or she has control.

What makes a good evaluation technique? Ideally, a measure of a firm's performance should consider several factors. First, the measure should not be sensitive to the choice of accounting methods. Second, the measure should evaluate the firm's current decisions in light of the expected future results. Third, the measure should consider the risk associated with the decisions made by the firm. Fourth, the measure should neither penalize nor reward the firm's management for factors outside its control, such as market movements and unanticipated changes in the economy. We will look at these criteria when discussing the particulars of the measures in the next two chapters.

Summary

The purpose of this tutorial is to examine traditional and recently developed measures of performance and to compare these measures with the market's assessment of company performance. We examine several traditional measures of company performance in Chapter 2 and more recently devised measures in Chapter 3. We compare these measures empirically with market performance measures in Chapter 4 and offer concluding remarks in Chapter 5.

A disclaimer that we should reveal up-front is that these recently devised methods, although steeped in traditional corporate theory, are proprietary methods. Therefore, we cannot replicate the precise details of application. Furthermore, each of these methods is used in application not only to judge firm performance as a whole but to provide assessment of divisional or product line management. We do not purport to replicate these methods precisely or demonstrate how these methods are applied within a corporation to evaluate management performance, but rather, we give a general descriptive overview and an empirical approximation. We hope that by providing the tools to critique performance measures, the analyst will be able to evaluate methods in a particular application.

2. Traditional Measures of Performance

A number of financial ratios are traditionally used to evaluate a firm's performance. These measures include return-on-investment and market-to-book (expressed by Tobin's q) ratios. In this chapter, we take a brief look at each of these ratios and how they are used to evaluate performance.

Return-on-Investment Ratios

Return-on-investment ratios compare the benefit from decisions (represented in the numerator) with the resources affecting that benefit (represented in the denominator). To evaluate how well the firm uses its assets in its operations, the *basic earning power ratio*, the ratio of earnings before interest and taxes (i.e., operating earnings) to total assets, can be used:

$$\text{Basic earning power ratio} = \frac{\text{Earnings before interest and taxes}}{\text{Total assets}}. \tag{2.1}$$

For example, a basic earning power ratio of 25 percent means that for every dollar invested in assets, the firm generates 25 cents of operating profit. Because this measure deals with earnings from operations, it does not consider how these operations are financed; that is, the earnings before interest and taxes are available to pay both creditors and owners.

Another return-on-investment ratio, *return on assets*, uses net income (i.e., operating earnings less interest and taxes) in comparison with total assets:

$$\text{Return on assets} = \frac{\text{Net income}}{\text{Total assets}}. \tag{2.2}$$

This ratio shows the return available to owners from the investment of capital from both creditors and owners. A return on assets of 20 percent indicates that for every dollar of capital, a profit of 20 cents is generated for the firm's owners.

An investor may not be interested in the return the firm gets from its total investment (that is, the funds provided by both creditors and owners), but rather, he or she may be interested in the return the firm earns on the equity investment. For example, common shareholders are interested in the return the firm can generate on their investment. *Return on equity* is the ratio of the net income shareholders receive to their equity in the stock:

$$\text{Return on equity} = \frac{\text{Net income}}{\text{Book value of equity}}. \tag{2.3}$$

A return on equity of 10 percent indicates that for every dollar invested by owners (as reflected in book-value terms), they earn 10 cents.

Generally, higher return ratios are associated with better performance. Return ratios are typically used in two ways. First, return ratios are often compared over time for a given firm if it is the trend, rather than the actual return for a particular period, that indicates performance. Second, return ratios are often compared among firms or compared with a benchmark, such as an industry average return or a return for the industry leaders.

An advantage of using return ratios in evaluating a firm's performance is the ease of calculation. All information necessary for the calculation is readily available, either from financial statements or from market data. And because the return is expressed as a percentage of the investment, its interpretation is straightforward.

An attractive feature of return ratios is that they can be decomposed to reveal the sources of changes in returns. For example, a low return on assets may be attributable to low activity, low margins, or both. When evaluating past operating performance to investigate different aspects of the management of the firm or to predict future performance, knowing the source of these returns is valuable information. *DuPont analysis* is used to look at return ratios by breaking the return ratios into their activity and profit components.[1] This technique allows for further evaluating the source of the return changes from year to year and for evaluating differences among firms.

Return-on-investment measures are not good measures of performance for a number of reasons. First, the return-on-investment ratios are formed using financial statement data in the numerator and/or the denominator; therefore, these ratios are sensitive to the choice of accounting methods. This sensitivity to accounting methods makes comparing return ratios among firms and over time difficult, thereby requiring an adjustment of the accounting data to place return ratios on the same accounting basis.

Second, these ratios use financial data that are an accumulation of monetary values from different time periods. For example, the gross plant account includes the cost of assets purchased at different points in time. If significant inflation takes place in some periods, an "apples and oranges" addition problem results for most accounts, which affects total assets and equity and distorts the calculated return on investment.

Third, return-on-investment ratios are backward looking, not forward looking. Although the immediate effects of current investments influence the return ratios, the expected future benefits from current-period decisions are generally not incorporated in the return ratios.

A fourth deficiency of return-on-investment ratios is that they fail to consider risk. These ratios simply use historical financial statement data that in no way reflect the uncertainty the firm faces.

Finally, the return-on-investment ratios do not adjust for controllable versus noncontrollable factors. Ideally, the performance of the firm should be isolated from factors that are outside the control of management. Yet, the return-on-investment ratios reflect the bottom line alone and do not consider any other factors.

Tobin's *q*

Tobin's *q* is often used as a measure of the real value created by a firm's management.[2] The higher the *q*, the more value is added. The attractiveness of *q* is that it provides an estimate of the firm's intangible assets, which include market power, goodwill, quality management, and future investment opportunities; the greater the value of these intangibles, the greater the value of *q*. Therefore, ranking firms on the basis of

---

[1]The decomposition of return ratios in terms of profit margin and turnover ratios is credited to E.I. duPont de Nemours & Company, whose management developed a system of breaking down return ratios into their components (American Management Association 1960).

[2]Tobin's *q* is named for its originator, James Tobin (Tobin 1969).

their *q*-values amounts to ranking firms on the basis of anticipated future cash flow generation. Furthermore, looking at changes in *q*-values from year to year gives an analyst an idea of how the firm's opportunities have changed.

The *q*-value is the ratio of the market value of a firm's assets to the replacement value of its assets:

$$q = \frac{\text{Market value of assets}}{\text{Replacement cost of assets}}. \qquad (2.4)$$

The greater the real return on investment (that is, the return after the effects of inflation), the greater the value of *q*.

The estimation of the replacement cost of assets is fairly difficult. One approximation was proposed by Lindenberg and Ross (1981). In this approximation, the numerator is the sum of the book value of debt (adjusted for age), market value of common equity, and book value of preferred stock, less net short-term assets. The denominator is total assets plus an adjustment for inflation on the firm's equity capital. These calculations can be quite complex with respect to the debt adjustment and the inflation adjustment.

An alternative proxy for Tobin's *q* is a ratio whose numerator comprises both market value (common stock) and book value (preferred stock and debt):

$$\text{Proxy for } q = \frac{\substack{\text{Book value} \\ \text{of debt}} + \substack{\text{Liquidating value} \\ \text{of preferred stock}} + \substack{\text{Market value of} \\ \text{common stock}}}{\text{Total assets}}. \qquad (2.5)$$

This proxy has been shown to be empirically close to the more complex Lindenberg and Ross proxy (Chung and Pruitt 1994; Perfect and Wiles 1994). For example, Perfect and Wiles compare five different proxies, ranging from the very complex to the simplest, and find that these proxies differ somewhat when comparing *q*-values for firms but are not substantially different when looking at changes in *q*-values.

This *q*-proxy resembles the market-to-book ratio except that the book value of debt and the liquidating value of preferred stock are included in both the numerator and the denominator. The close relation between the proxy for the *q*-ratio (which has theoretical underpinnings) and the book-to-market equity ratio may explain why the latter has been shown to explain security returns.

Many researchers observe that the ratio of the book value of equity to the market value of equity (BV/MV) is related to security returns: High BV/MVs are associated with high future returns.[3,4] For example, Fama and French (1992) find that BV/MV and firm size (i.e., equity capitalization) explain cross-sectional security returns. Furthermore, they find that BV/MV explains security returns better than both beta and size: High-BV/MV firms have high returns.

Why the book-to-market equity ratio explains security returns is not known because little theoretical justification exists for this ratio to influence returns. Several explana-

---

[3]See, for example, Rosenberg, Reid, and Lanstein (1985); Chan, Hamao, and Lakonishok (1990); Fama and French (1992, 1995); and Harris and Marston (1994).

[4]The relation between the market value of equity and the book value of equity is used by some in the form of MV/BV and by others in the form of the inverse, BV/MV. We use the form MV/BV to simplify the interpretation of the analysis and comparison with other performance measures: Higher is better. This statement does not mean that high-MV/BV firms will outperform low-MV/BV firms in the future. Evidence indicates that high-MV/BV firms ("growth" firms) will underperform low-MV/BV firms ("value" firms) in the future.

tions for the role of BV/MV exist. One explanation is that BV/MV is a proxy for risk: The greater the firm's BV/MV, the greater the risk of that firm's security. This explanation is consistent with the efficient market theory and Fama and French's evidence if BV/MV is considered a risk factor and is, therefore, priced accordingly.

Another explanation for the book-to-market ratio's relation to security returns is that it proxies for future growth: The greater the BV/MV, the lower the firm's expected future growth prospects. This explanation is supported by Harris and Marston (1994).[5] Given this explanation, the ratio is a measure of the value added by the firm's management: The lower the value of this ratio, the better the firm is managing its assets to generate future value for the firm.

Related to this explanation is the hypothesis offered by Haugen (1995): The market consistently overestimates the persistence of above-average future growth, which explains why low-BV/MV firms underperform high-BV/MV firms. This argument is supported by Lakonishok, Shleifer, and Vishny (1994), who observe that the earnings growth rates tend to converge for high-BV/MV and low-BV/MV securities and that the market tends to overextrapolate earnings growth.

The relation among BV/MV, Tobin's q, and security returns is straightforward:

Statement 1: Firms that currently have high BV–MV ratios tend to have higher future returns than firms with low BV–MV ratios. Hence, selecting firms on the basis of BV/MV may produce superior returns.

Statement 2: Firms with current high values of q (hence, low BV/MV) tend to be those firms that have performed well in terms of past stock returns, because the greater stock value is reflected in q's numerator (Equation 2.5).

Are these statements in conflict? Not necessarily. Firms with high q-values (low BV/MVs) have added value relative to book capital. The higher the q, the better the firm's *past* performance, which does not mean that these firms will necessarily produce superior returns in the future. In fact, if Haugen's explanation of mean-reverting growth is true, high-q firms may have performed well in the past but may not necessarily perform well in the future, which points out a problem with Tobin's q and other traditional measures: Performance in the past does not necessarily indicate performance in the future. Therefore, these measures may not be useful in portfolio selection, even though they may be useful to gauge current and past performance.

Summary

The traditional measures of firm performance are based largely on accounting data; therefore, any use of these measures must consider the potential distortions arising from the chosen accounting methods. In addition, these traditional measures use, for the most part, historical data to measure current performance. Ideally, one would like to measure how current decisions will affect the firm's future performance.

However one may criticize the traditional measures of performance, the key to their use is whether they are sufficient measures of performance. We take an empirical look at these traditional measures in Chapter 4 and examine how well several of the measures relate firm performance to stock return measures of performance.

---

[5]Still another explanation is that high-BV/MV securities are underpriced; hence, subsequent returns are higher for high-BV/MV stocks. This explanation, however, is sufficient only if the market is inefficient. This explanation is not supported by Harris and Marston (1994), among others.

3. Measures of Value Added

Measuring whether a firm's management has increased or decreased a firm's value during a period is difficult because a firm's value may be affected by many factors. Currently advocated performance measurement techniques, such as Stern, Stewart & Company's EVA and MVA approaches, are based on valuation principles, but an important distinction exists between valuation and performance measurement: Valuation relies on forecasts, and performance measurement relies on actual results. In this chapter, we take a close look at value-added measures of performance and discuss an alternative measure of performance, the cash flow return on investment (CFROI).

Economic Profit

Many U.S. corporations, including The Coca-Cola Company, Briggs & Stratton Corporation, CSX Corporation, and AT&T Corporation, are embracing a relatively new method of evaluating and rewarding management performance that is based on the idea of compensating management for economic profit rather than for accounting profit.[1] What is economic profit? It is basically the difference between revenues and costs, where the costs include not only expenses but also the cost of capital. And although the application of economic profit is relatively new in the measurement of performance, the concept of economic profit has been around since the late 19th century (Marshall 1890). What this recent emphasis on economic profit has done is focus attention away from accounting profit and toward the cost of capital.[2]

The *cost of capital* is the rate of return that is required by the suppliers of a firm's capital. For a business that finances its operations or investments using both debt and equity, the cost of capital includes the explicit interest on the debt and the implicit minimum return that owners require. This minimum return to owners is necessary so that owners will keep their investment capital in the firm.

Economic Profit versus Accounting Profit. Two important distinctions must be made between accounting profit and economic profit. The first distinction deals with the cost of capital. Accounting profit is the difference between revenues and costs, based on the representation of these items according to accounting principles. Economic profit is also the difference between revenues and costs, but unlike in the determination of accounting profit, in economic profit, the cost of capital is included in the costs.

The second distinction between accounting and economic profit deals with the principles of recognition of revenues and costs. Accounting profits, for the most part, are represented using the accrual method, whereas economic profits reflect cash-basis accounting. But because the data reported in financial statements are only in terms of accrual accounting, analysts calculating economic profits must first start with accounting profits and then make adjustments to place the data on a cash basis. Further

---

[1]One of the first people to advocate using economic profit in compensating management was Stewart (1991).

[2]For a discussion of the benefits from this shift in focus, see, for example, Rutledge (1993), Stern (1993a, 1993b, 1994), Sheehan (1994), Jones (1995), and Saint (1995).

adjustments must be made to accounting profits to compensate for distortions that may arise from the choice of particular accounting methods. For example, goodwill is amortized over 40 years in the United States, but goodwill does not represent a cost; goodwill amortization must thus be added back into reported net income in calculating economic profit.

Unlike accounting profit, economic profit (if measured accurately) cannot be manipulated by management through the choice of accounting methods. Furthermore, basing compensation on economic profit, rather than accounting profit, encourages longer-sighted decision making. Therefore, management compensation based on economic profit is an attractive idea.

In addition to the use of economic profit for compensating managers, financial analysts are incorporating the basic principles of economic profit into their assessments of corporate success. Performance measures based on economic profit are known by several names, including MVA and EVA approaches and excess shareholder value.

Economic Profit and Net Present Value. The estimation of economic profit is analogous to the net present value method of evaluating investments. Although the concept is attractive in principle, many pitfalls are associated with how economic profit applies the net present value capital-budgeting technique to actual firms. These pitfalls involve (1) the use of accounting data to determine economic profit and (2) the estimation of the cost of capital.[3]

Just as the net present value of a project produces results that are sensitive to the cost of capital, so does the economic profit approach. For example, if the cost of capital for Anheuser-Busch Companies is estimated at 11.3 percent, the economic value added for 1992 is $235 million (Tully 1993). On the other hand, if the cost of capital is estimated at, say, 12 percent, the economic value added for the same year is $179 million. The slight difference in the cost-of-capital estimate changes the estimated value added by $56 million. The variation in the cost-of-capital estimate may also change the resulting compensation for Anheuser-Busch's management.

Economic profit is an idea that has been around for a long time and is based on the concepts of valuation advocated for many years in academia. In most introductory textbooks on finance, the net present value method that is used to evaluate capital projects is presented in detail.[4] In the case of a capital project, the net present value is the present value of future expected cash flows from a particular investment in which these cash flows are discounted at the cost of capital. The net present value, hence, represents the incremental value that the project adds to the firm. When compared with alternative methods of evaluating capital projects, the net present value method is found to be superior to the other commonly used techniques: the internal rate of return (IRR) and payback period methods.

The net present value method as applied in the context of evaluating performance of firms and management was brought to prominence by G. Bennett Stewart III in his book entitled *The Quest for Value*, which was published in 1991, and through the consulting work of Stern Stewart & Company.

Calculation of Economic Profit. Economic profit, referred to as economic value added, is the difference between operating profits and the cost of capital, where the cost of capital is expressed in dollar terms. The application of this technique to an entire

---

[3]The cost of capital is an opportunity cost of funds, measured as the weighted average of the marginal costs of debt and equity capital.

[4]See, for example, Peterson (1994, Chapter 9) and Brigham (1995, Chapter 9).

firm involves, essentially, calculating the net present value of all investment projects, both those involving existing assets (i.e., past investment decisions) and projected investments. Economic profit can, according to Stewart (1991, p. 136), be written as

$$\text{Economic profit} = \text{Net operating profit after taxes} - (\text{Cost of capital} \times \text{Capital}) \qquad (3.1)$$

or, equivalently, using the spread between the rate of return and the percentage cost of capital,

$$\text{Economic profit} = (\text{Return on capital} - \text{Cost of capital}) \times \text{Capital}, \qquad (3.2)$$

where the *return on capital* is the ratio of net operating profit after taxes (NOPAT) to capital.[5]

Applying this formula produces an estimate of the economic profit for a single period. In evaluating a firm's performance for a given period, economic profit reflects whether value is added (a positive economic profit) or reduced (a negative economic profit). Following is a detailed discussion of each element contained in this formula.

■ *NOPAT.* Two elements are important in the calculation of NOPAT: operating profit after depreciation and cash operating taxes. Cash operating taxes are taxes on operating income, placed on a cash basis.

Operating income *after* depreciation is used rather than the traditional operating income *before* depreciation because depreciation is considered an economic expense: Depreciation is a measure of how much of an asset is used up in the period, which indicates how much must be expended to maintain operations at the existing level. In addition to cash operating taxes, several adjustments that are intended to alter accounting profit to better reflect economic profit need to be made, but because these adjustments involve modifying accounting profit to arrive at economic profit, they must be tailored to the firm's specific accounting practices and situation. Adjustments noted by Stewart (1991) to arrive at NOPAT are detailed in Table 3.1. As shown in this table, whether starting with operating profit after depreciation (the "bottom-up" approach) or beginning with sales (the "top-down" approach), one arrives at adjusted operating profit before taxes. Subtracting cash operating taxes from the adjusted profit produces NOPAT.

To show how adjustments are made to actual company data, we will calculate NOPAT for Hershey Foods Corporation for 1993. Using the basic income statement data as presented in Table 3.2 and footnote information (not shown in table) and applying the bottom-up approach, we begin with operating profit after depreciation and amortization of $457.228 million.

The adjustments applicable to Hershey include[6]
- implied interest on operating leases (implied from future rental commitments, as detailed in *Hershey Foods Corporation 1993 Annual Report*, footnote 13);
- increase in LIFO reserve, $10.663 million (*Hershey Foods Corporation 1993 Annual Report*, footnote 14); and
- goodwill amortization, $12.200 million (*Hershey Foods Corporation 1993 Annual Report*, footnote 1).

---

[5]The cost of capital times capital is the cost of capital in dollar terms. The return on capital minus the cost of capital is the spread.

[6]Information on change in the bad-debt reserve and capitalized research and development is not available in Hershey's financial statement. Therefore, these adjustments are not made, which points to a potential problem in calculating economic profit: The information needed may not be available in published financial reports.

Table 3.1. Calculation of NOPAT from Financial Statement Data

A. Bottom-up approach

Begin:
    Operating profit after depreciation and amortization

Add:
    Implied interest expense on operating leases
    Increase in LIFO reserve
    Goodwill amortization
    Increase in bad-debt reserve
    Increase in net capitalized research and development

Equals:
    Adjusted operating profit before taxes

Subtract:
    Cash operating taxes

Equals:
    NOPAT

B. Top-down approach

Begin:
    Sales

Add:
    Increase in LIFO reserve
    Implied interest expense on operating leases
    Other income

Subtract:
    Cost of goods sold
    Selling, general, and administrative expenses
    Depreciation

Equals:
    Adjusted operating profit before taxes

Subtract:
    Cash operating taxes

Equals:
    NOPAT

Note: Table based on information in Stewart (1991).

Therefore, most of the information needed to calculate NOPAT is available directly from the financial statements or the footnotes to financial statements. An exception is the implied interest expense on operating leases, which must be calculated using footnote information. The interest expense is estimated as the interest cost on the change in the average value of leases during the year, which requires estimating the present value of leases at the beginning and end of the year.

The present value of operating leases is determined by discounting minimum rental commitments on operating leases for the next five years. These minimum rental commitments are disclosed in a footnote to the financial statements. In the case of Hershey, the expected future commitments beyond 1993 are as follows:

Year Relative to 1993	Operating Lease Rental Commitment (millions)
First year	$ 12.3
Second year	12.0
Third year	11.4
Fourth year	11.1
Fifth year	10.7
Beyond the fifth year	102.8

With a discount rate of 7.1 percent (the yield on Hershey's debt in 1993), the present value of the first five years of commitments is $47.256 million. With the rental commitments estimated at $10 million a year following the fifth year, the present value of the operating leases increases to $147.209 million.[7] Because many financial statements provide information on only the next five years, the value of the commitments beyond the fifth year is often ignored in the determination of capital. In the case of Hershey, ignoring commitments beyond the fifth year amounts to a difference of approximately $100 million in debt capital.

Repeating the same analysis for 1992 using a discount rate of 8.1 percent produces a present value of the operating leases of $126.904 million. The average lease value for 1993 is, therefore, $137.057 million [($147.209 million + $126.904 million)/2]. With an interest rate of 7.1 percent, the interest on the leases is $9.731 million. This implied interest is backed out of operating profit because it represents a financing cost that is deducted to arrive at reported operating profit.

Starting with the operating profit after depreciation and amortization from the 1993 income statement, adjusted operating profit before taxes for Hershey is calculated as

	Amount (millions)
Operating profit after depreciation and amortization	$457.228
Add: Implied interest on operating leases	9.731
Add: Increase in LIFO reserve	10.663
Add: Goodwill amortization	12.200
Adjusted operating profit before taxes	$489.822

■ *Cash operating taxes.* Cash operating taxes are estimated by starting with the income tax expense and adjusting this expense for (1) changes in deferred taxes, (2) the tax benefit from the interest deduction (for explicit and implicit interest) to remove the tax effect of financing with debt, and (3) taxes from other nonoperating income or expenses and special items.[8] The change in deferred taxes is removed from the income tax expense for the following reasons:

• An increase in deferred taxes means that a portion of the income tax expense that is deferred is not a cash outlay for the period.

• A decrease in deferred taxes means that the income tax expense understates the true cash expense.

The tax benefit from interest is added back to taxes so that the cash taxes reflect the taxes from operations; this gross up of taxes isolates the taxes from any financing effects. This tax benefit is the reduction of taxes from the deductibility of interest expense:

$$\text{Tax benefit from interest} = \text{Interest expense} \times \text{Marginal tax rate.}$$

The taxes from other nonoperating income and special items (sales of investment interest) are also removed so that the cash taxes reflect solely those taxes related to operations.

---

[7]The present value of the perpetuity of $10 million each year forever is $140.845 million. Discounting this value to 1993 prices at 7.1 percent adds $99.953 million to the present value of the leases.

[8]The adjustment for the taxes on other nonoperating income is suggested by Copeland, Koller, and Murrin (1994), although the amount is typically small.

Table 3.2. Hershey's Financial Statements
    (millions)

	1993	1992
A. Balance sheet		
Assets		
Cash and cash equivalents	$ 15.959	$ 203.190
Net receivable	294.974	173.646
Inventories	453.442	457.179
Other current assets	124.621	105.966
Total current assets	$ 888.996	$ 939.981
Gross plant, property, and equipment	$2,041.764	$1,797.437
Accumulated depreciation	580.860	501.448
Net plant, property, and equipment	$1,460.904	$1,295.989
Intangibles	473.408	399.768
Other assets	31.783	37.171
Total assets	$2,855.091	$2,672.909
Liabilities		
Long-term debt due in one year	$ 13.309	$104.224
Notes payable	354.486	281.045
Accounts payable	108.458	105.175
Taxes payable	35.603	5.682
Accrued expenses	301.989	240.816
Total current liabilities	$813.845	$736.942
Long-term debt	$165.757	$174.273
Deferred taxes	172.744	203.465
Other liabilities	290.401	92.950
Equity		
Common stock	$ 89.922	$ 90.186
Capital surplus	9.681	7.421
Retained earnings	1,431.704	1,367.672
Less Treasury stock	118.963	0.000
Common equity	$1,412.344	$1,465.279
Total liabilities and equity	$2,855.091	$2,672.909
B. Income statement		
Sales	$3,488.249	$3,219.805
Cost of goods sold	1,895.378	1,748.954
Gross profit	1,592.871	1,470.851
Selling and general administrative expense	1,035.519	958.189
Operating income before depreciation and amortization	$ 557.352	$ 512.662
Depreciation and amortization	100.124	84.434
Operating profit	$ 457.228	$ 428.228
Interest expense	34.870	41.763
Nonoperating income and expense	7.875	14.523
Special items	80.642	0.000
Pretax income	$ 510.875	$ 400.988
Total income taxes	213.642	158.390
Income before extraordinary items	297.233	242.598
Extraordinary items	(103.908)	0.000
Net income	$ 193.325	$ 242.598

Source: *Hershey Foods Corporation 1993 Annual Report.*

Following is an example of calculating cash operating taxes using Hershey's 1993 financial data. First, we calculate cash taxes using a marginal tax rate of 35 percent:

	Amount (millions)	Source of Data
Income tax expense	$213.642	Income statement
Add: Decrease in deferred taxes	30.721	Difference between deferred taxes on balance sheets for 1993 and 1992
Add: Tax benefit from interest expense	12.205	Interest expense from income statement times the marginal tax rate
Add: Tax benefit from interest on leases	3.406	Implied interest from footnote information times marginal tax rate
Less: Taxes on nonoperating income	(2.756)	Nonoperating income from income statement times marginal tax rate
Less: Taxes on special items	(40.000)	Calculated from footnote 3
Cash operating taxes	$217.218	

Subtracting cash operating taxes from the adjusted operating profit produces NOPAT:

	Amount (millions)
Adjusted operating profit before taxes	$489.822
Less: Cash operating taxes	(217.218)
NOPAT	$272.604

This approach to calculating NOPAT is a bottom-up approach because it starts with operating profit after depreciation and amortization and builds to NOPAT. Another approach is a top-down approach: starting with sales and adjusting to arrive at NOPAT. In the case of Hershey for 1993,

	Amount (millions)	Source of Information
Sales	$3,488.249	Income statement
Less: Cost of goods sold	(1,895.378)	Income statement
Less: Selling, general, and administrative expenses	(1,035.519)	Income statement
Less: Depreciation	(87.924)	Depreciation and amortization from income statement, less goodwill amortization from footnote 1
Add: Implied interest on operating leases	9.731	Calculated from footnote 13
Add: Increase in LIFO reserve	10.663	Calculated from footnote 14
Adjusted operating profit before taxes	$ 489.822	
Less: Cash operating taxes	(217.218)	
NOPAT	$ 272.604	

Whether using the top-down or the bottom-up approach, NOPAT is calculated to be $272.604 million.

■ *Capital.* Capital is defined in this context as the sum of net working capital, net property and equipment, goodwill, and other assets. Several adjustments to reported accounts are made to correct for possible distortions arising from accounting methods. For example, inventory is adjusted for any LIFO reserve; the present value of operating leases is included; and accumulated goodwill amortization is added to capital. Table 3.3 shows a list of potential adjustments to capital. One approach to estimating capital is the *asset approach*—begin with net operating assets and then make adjustments to reflect total invested capital, as shown in Panel A of Table 3.3. For example, the goodwill generated from paying more for acquiring a company than the book value of its assets can be considered to be an investment; therefore, both goodwill and prior periods' amortization of goodwill are added to reflect the firm's asset investment. Another approach, the *source of financing approach*, begins with the book value of common equity and adds debt, equity equivalents, and debt equivalents, as detailed in Panel B of Table 3.3.

Perusing the footnotes of the financial statements is necessary to arrive at these adjustments, and the calculation of capital should, ideally, be tailored to reflect each firm's financial accounting. Also notice that in Tables 3.1 and 3.3, the adjustments made to arrive at NOPAT have companion adjustments to arrive at capital. And as with the NOPAT calculations, capital can be calculated by starting at either of two points: total assets (the asset approach) or book value of equity (sources of financing approach).

Continuing the example using Hershey, capital calculated using the asset approach is[9]

	Amount (millions)	Source of Information
Begin with net operating assets[a]	$ 442.946	Current assets, less accounts payable, taxes payable, and accrued expenses—all from the balance sheet
Add: LIFO reserve	59.005	Footnote 14
Add: Net plant, property, and equipment	1,460.904	Balance sheet
Add: Other assets	31.783	Balance sheet
Add: Goodwill	473.408	Balance sheet (assumption: all intangibles represent goodwill)
Add: Accumulated goodwill amortization	73.400	Footnote 1
Add: Present value of operating leases	147.209	Implied from data in footnote 13
Capital	$2,688.655	

[a]Operating current assets include cash, marketable securities, receivables, inventories, and other current assets; for Hershey in 1993, the amount was $888.996 million. Net operating assets are operating current assets less accounts payable, taxes payable, and accrued expenses.

Alternatively, starting with the book value of equity,

	Amount (millions)	Source of Information
Begin with book value of equity	$1,412.344	Balance sheet
Add: Deferred income tax reserve	172.744	Balance sheet
Add: LIFO reserve	59.005	Footnote 14
Add: Accumulated goodwill amortization	73.400	Footnote 1
Equity and equity equivalents	$1,717.493	
Add: Book value of long-term debt	179.066	Current and long-term portions of debt from balance sheet
Add: Interest-bearing short-term debt	354.486	Notes payable from balance sheet
Add: Present value of operating leases	147.209	Calculated from footnote 13
Add: Other liabilities	290.401	Balance sheet
Debt and debt equivalents	971.162	
Capital	$2,688.655	

Copeland, Koller, and Murrin (1994) make a further distinction between invested capital (as described earlier) and operating capital. Operating capital is invested capital less goodwill, excess cash, and marketable securities, that is, capital used in operations.

[9]Information on bad-debt reserve, capitalized research and development, and cumulative write-offs was not available in the financial statements. The extent to which these omissions affect the resultant measure of economic value added is unknown, but these items are also omitted in published examples of economic value added because of unavailability of the data (see, for example, the explanations accompanying the Wal-Mart example in Stewart [1991, p. 99]).

Table 3.3. Calculation of Capital Using Accounting Financial Statements

A. Asset approach
Begin:
    Net operating assets
Add:
    LIFO reserve
    Net plant and equipment
    Other assets
    Goodwill
    Accumulated goodwill amortization
    Present value of operating leases
    Bad-debt reserve
    Capitalized research and development
    Cumulative write-offs of special items
Equals:
    Capital

B. Source of financing approach
Begin:
    Book value of common equity
Add equity equivalents:
    Preferred stock
    Minority interest
    Deferred income tax reserve
    LIFO reserve
    Accumulated goodwill amortization
Add debt and debt equivalents:
    Interest-bearing short-term debt
    Long-term debt
    Capitalized lease obligations
    Present value of noncapitalized leases
Equals:
    Capital

Note: Table based on information in Stewart (1991).

Goodwill is removed from capital because it tends to be distorted by premiums paid in acquiring other companies. Excess cash and marketable securities are those in excess of the typical need for cash and marketable securities. Copeland, Koller, and Murrin (1994, pp. 160–61) estimate that the need for cash and marketable securities is between 0.5 percent and 2 percent of sales, varying by industry. In 1993, cash and marketable securities were $15.959 million for Hershey, or less than 0.01 percent of sales. Therefore, no adjustment for excess cash and marketable securities need be made. Goodwill for Hershey in 1993 was $473.408 million, and accumulated goodwill amortization was $73.400 million. Removing goodwill (and accumulated amortization) from invested capital produces operating capital of $2,141.847 million.

    ■ *Return on capital.* The return on capital is operating income after taxes divided by capital. This measure is a return-on-investment measure that uses NOPAT instead of accounting profit:

$$\text{Return on capital} = \frac{\text{Net operating profit after taxes}}{\text{Capital}}. \qquad (3.3)$$

For example, the return on capital for Hershey is the ratio of NOPAT to invested capital, or

$$\text{Hershey's return on capital} = \frac{\$272.604 \text{ million}}{\$2,688.655 \text{ million}}$$
$$= 10.139\%.$$

The return on operating capital for Hershey is

$$\text{Hershey's return on operating capital} = \frac{\$272.604 \text{ million}}{\$2,141.847 \text{ million}}$$
$$= 12.728\% .$$

Which return measure is best to use when evaluating Hershey? The answer depends on whether the focus is on (1) Hershey's ability to profitably and efficiently use investors' funds (including funds used to acquire other firms at a premium), which requires use of the former measure, or (2) Hershey's ability to profitably and efficiently use its operating assets (allowing better comparability among firms in the same industry), which requires the use of the latter measure.

■ *Cost of capital.* The cost of capital is the cost of raising additional funds from debt and equity sources. A cost is associated with each source. Once the cost of each source is determined, the cost of capital for the firm is calculated as a weighted average of each cost, where the weight represents the proportionate use of each source. The traditional method of estimating the cost of capital is detailed in Appendix A.

The cost of debt is the after-tax cost of debt, r_d^*, which is the before-tax cost adjusted for the benefit from the tax deductibility of interest:

$$r_d^* = r_d \times (1 - \text{Marginal corporate tax rate}), \tag{3.4}$$

where the before-tax rate, r_d, is the prevailing yield on long-term bonds of firms with similar credit risk. For example, in 1993, bonds of similar risk to Hershey's bonds yielded an average of 7.4 percent. Using the marginal tax rate of 35 percent, the after-tax cost of debt for Hershey is

$$r_d^* = 0.074(1 - 0.35)$$
$$= 4.8\% .$$

The cost of equity capital is the sum of the risk-free rate of interest and the risk premium:

$$r_e = r_f + \beta(r_m - r_f), \tag{3.5}$$

where r_f is the risk-free rate of interest, r_m is the expected return on the market, and β is the capital asset pricing model (CAPM) beta.

This calculation is not as straightforward as it looks. One issue is the appropriate proxy for the risk-free rate. The risk-free rate of interest should, theoretically, be the return on a zero-beta portfolio that has a duration similar to the holding period of the investor. Because calculating such a rate is extremely difficult, an alternative is to proxy the risk-free rate using rates on securities with no default risk, that is, U.S. government debt. If a government obligation with a short duration is used, such as a Treasury bill, a mismatch in the duration between the Treasury bill and the risk-free portfolio occurs. A more suitable proxy would be a 10-year government bond because it matches the duration of the market portfolio.[10] Stewart (1991) specifies that this rate should be the rate on a long-term government bond. Copeland, Koller, and Murrin are more specific and advocate the rate on a 10-year U.S. Treasury bond. With the latter approach, the risk-free rate for 1993 is 5.87 percent.

[10]See Copeland, Koller, and Murrin (1994, Chapter 8) for a discussion of the comparability of durations.

Another issue is the premium for market risk, $r_m - r_f$. Stewart advocates a 6 percent market risk premium, which is based on the historical spread between the return on the market and the return on long-term government bonds. Copeland, Koller, and Murrin advocate the use of the difference between the geometric mean return on the market and that of long-term government bonds, both calculated over a long time frame. The estimates using 1926–93 data produce a market risk premium of 5 percent.[11]

The market risk premium is tailored to the company's specific risk premium by multiplying the market risk premium by the firm's common stock beta, β. Beta is a measure of the sensitivity of the returns on the firm's stock to changes in the returns on the market and is readily available from financial services such as BARRA, Standard & Poor's Compustat, or the *Value Line Investment Survey*. Hershey's beta is 1.0.[12] With the 10-year Treasury bond rate, a market risk premium of 5 percent, and a beta of 1.0, Hershey's cost of equity is

$$r_e = 0.0587 + 1.0(0.05)$$
$$= 10.87\% .$$

Using a market risk premium of 6 percent produces a higher cost of capital, 11.87 percent.

In summation, Hershey's cost of capital is composed of the cost of debt of 4.8 percent and the cost of equity of 10.87 percent (or for an alternative risk premium, 11.87 percent). The costs of debt and equity are weighted using the proportions each represents in the capital structure to arrive at a cost of capital for the firm.

The first step to calculating cost of capital is to determine the book values of debt and equity. The debt and equity book values can be taken from the calculation of capital. The second step is to estimate the market value of the capital components, which requires estimating the market values of debt and equity.

Hershey's capital structure at the end of 1993 consists of

Capital	Book Value (millions)	Market Value (millions)
Debt capital[a]	$ 971.162	$1,004.313
Equity capital	1,717.493	4,293.037
Total	$2,688.655	$5,297.350

[a]The market value of debt is estimated as the sum of the book value of long-term debt due in one year, notes payable at book value, the present value of operating leases (as calculated earlier), other liabilities at book value, and long-term debt at market value (as per *Moody's Bond Record*).

in dollar terms and

Capital	Book Value as a Percentage of Total Capital	Market Value as a Percentage of Total Capital
Debt capital	36.12%	18.96%
Equity capital	63.88	81.04
Total	100.00%	100.00%

---

[11]See Copeland, Koller, and Murrin (1994, pp. 260–61).
[12]The 1.0 beta taken from *Value Line* agrees with the beta reported by Compustat.

in terms of proportions.[13]

Hershey's capital structure at the end of 1992 (and the beginning of 1993) consists of

Capital	Book Value (millions)	Market Value (millions)
Debt capital	$ 779.396	$ 792.595
Equity capital	1,778.286	4,238.742
Total	$2,557.682	$5,031.337

in dollar terms and

Capital	Book Value (millions)	Market Value (millions)
Debt capital	30.473%	15.753%
Equity capital	69.527	84.247
Total	100.000%	100.000%

in terms of proportions.

Additions and subtractions to debt and equity capital are made throughout the year. Because of this fact and the lack of specific data on changes in capital, the capital proportions can be approximated by averaging the beginning and ending capital proportions for the year. Using book values yields approximately 33 percent debt and 67 percent equity. Hershey's weighted-average cost of capital (WACC) using the book weights and a 10.87 percent cost of equity is

$$\text{Hershey's WACC using book-value weights} = [0.33(0.048)] + [0.67(0.1087)]$$
$$= 0.0886 \text{ or } 8.86\%.$$

Using market-value weights, the cost of capital is greater because approximately 83 percent of Hershey's capital is equity:

$$\text{Hershey's WACC using market-value weights} = [0.17(0.048)] + [0.83(0.1087)]$$
$$= 0.0984 \text{ or } 9.84\%.$$

Which value should be used, 8.86 percent or 9.84 percent? For most applications, one should choose the method that better reflects the marginal cost of funds. If the firm raises an additional dollar of capital, in what proportion does it raise these funds? This question is usually thought of in terms of the market-value proportions—the 9.84 percent cost of capital. But in this particular application, the cost of capital is being applied against the invested capital, which is most often stated in terms of book values. Mixing a market-value-determined cost of capital with book value of invested capital results in distortions.[14] Therefore, the book-value-weighted cost of capital is used here to determine economic profit.

■ *Economic profit and performance*. Economic profit is the profit generated during the period in excess of what is required by investors for the level of risk associated with the firm's investments. Economic profit is analogous to the net present value of capital

---

[13]In addition to estimating the firm's most recent market value capital components, looking at the capital structure of other firms in the industry and considering the trends in the firm's capital structure over time are useful because the capital structure of a firm at a point in time may not reflect the firm's target capital structure.

[14]The extent of the distortion depends on the relation between the market value of capital and the book value of capital—in other words, the market-to-book value ratio discussed earlier.

budgeting and represents the value added by the firm's management during the period.

Using the two equivalent economic profit calculations shows that Hershey's management generated an economic profit in 1993:

$$\text{Hershey's economic profit} = \text{NOPAT} - (\text{Cost of capital} \times \text{Capital})$$
$$= \$272.604 \text{ million} - (0.0886 \times \$2,688.655 \text{ million})$$
$$= \$272.604 \text{ million} - \$238.215 \text{ million}$$
$$= \$34.389 \text{ million}$$

or

$$\text{Hershey's economic profit} = (\text{Rate of return} - \text{Cost of capital}) \times \text{Capital}$$
$$= (0.10139 - 0.0886) \times \$2,688.655 \text{ million}$$
$$= \$34.389 \text{ million}.$$

Hershey earned an economic profit of \$34.389 million in 1993. In other words, Hershey's management added value during 1993.

Although it seems that Hershey added value during the period, as represented by the estimate of economic profit, we should note that the estimate of economic profit is sensitive to the estimate of the cost of capital. The cost of capital is something that is difficult to measure, as noted in Appendix A. Looking at a range of cost of capital, plus and minus 100 basis points, gives an idea of this sensitivity:

$$\text{Hershey's economic profit if the cost of capital is 9.86\%} = \$272.604 \text{ million} - \$265.101 \text{ million}$$
$$= \$7.503 \text{ million.}$$

$$\text{Hershey's economic profit if the cost of capital is 7.86\%} = \$272.604 \text{ million} - \$211.328 \text{ million}$$
$$= \$61.276 \text{ million}$$

Consequently, drawing a conclusion regarding the degree of profitability depends, in large part, on the estimated cost of capital.

Market Value Added

A measure closely related to economic profit is market value added. Market value added is the difference between the firm's market value and its capital. Essentially, market value added is a measure of what the firm's management has been able to do with a given level of resources (the invested capital):

$$\text{Market value added} = \text{Market value of the firm} - \text{Capital.} \tag{3.6}$$

Like economic profit, market value added is expressed in terms of dollars, making the goal of the firm to increase added value. Performance is evaluated by looking at the *change* in market value added over a period. The change in the market value added is a measure of how effectively the firm's management uses capital to enhance its value for *all* suppliers of capital, not simply common shareholders.[15] The change in market value added is the change in the market value of capital (debt and equity) less the change in the book value of capital.

Looking once again at Hershey, the following can be seen for 1992 and 1993:

---

[15]A related issue is whether the firm's management should be striving to maximize the value of the firm or to maximize the value of common equity. The market-value-added measure focuses on the former, whereas more common measures, such as stock returns, focus on the latter. In general, maximizing the value of the firm will result in maximizing shareholder wealth.

Capital	1993 (millions)	1992 (millions)	Change from 1992 to 1993 (millions)
Market value of equity plus market value of debt	$5,297.350	$5,031.337	$266.013
Less: Invested capital	2,688.655	2,557.682	130.973
Market value added	$2,608.695	$2,473.655	$135.040

This analysis indicates that Hershey's management has increased market value added in 1993 by adding $135.040 million more in market value in excess of invested capital.[16]

In practice, the book value of debt and the book value of preferred stock are often used to estimate the market value of capital and the book value of capital.[17] Therefore, the change in market value added from one year to the next amounts to the change in the market value of common equity plus the change in the *book value* of debt and preferred stock.

Reconciling Economic Value Added with Market Value Added

Two approaches are used to measure value added: economic value added (economic profit) and market value added. Economic value added is based on adjusted operating earnings (after taxes), invested capital, and the firm's WACC. Market value added is based on a comparison of invested capital with the market value of capital. The two measures are both designed to help evaluate the performance of a firm.

Moreover, a logical link exists between market value added and economic profit. Market value added should be equal to the present value of future periods' economic profit discounted at the cost of capital. Assuming that the firm will generate, in perpetuity, future-period economic profit equivalent to the current period's economic profit, the relation between market value and economic profit is thus a simple one:

$$\text{Market value added} \approx \frac{\text{Economic profit}}{\text{Cost of capital}}. \tag{3.7}$$

The perpetuity assumption is not valid for most firms, however, because of a very basic notion: Economic profits are generated only when a firm has some comparative or competitive advantage. Most firms cannot maintain these advantages for long periods of time; for example, government regulations change, patents are not perpetual, and demographics change—all of which can erode a firm's advantage and, hence, its economic profit. Therefore, the assumption of a perpetual stream of the current period's economic profit is not reasonable in most cases.

Another reason why the relation in Equation 3.7 does not hold in practice is that the methods of determining economic profit and market value added are quite different. Economic value added is a single-period measure that is estimated using accounting data and an estimated cost of capital. Market value added uses market values, which are more forward-looking estimates of performance than economic profit.

A final reason why Equation 3.7 does not hold true is that the estimates of economic

---

[16]In the case of Hershey, a small portion of the value added is from the increase in the market value of existing debt that resulted from a change in bond yields. The change in bond yields, which is in general outside the control of Hershey's management, thus affects the estimate of market value added (and, for that matter, economic profit, through the cost of capital). This sensitivity to changes in yields is, therefore, a weakness of economic profit and market value added; factors outside the control of the firm's management affect the performance measure.

[17]See, for example, Stewart (1991, pp. 153–54).

©The Research Foundation of the ICFA

profit are just that—estimates. Economic profit is estimated by starting with accounting data and making adjustments to better reflect economic reality. No matter how careful an analyst is in adjusting the accounting data, the estimated economic profit cannot precisely reflect true economic profit.

Economic profit and market value added may result in conflicting evaluations of performance. For example, in 1993, General Electric Company ranked fourth among 1,000 firms selected by Stern Stewart based on its market value added ($42 billion), which indicates that General Electric was one of the best firms in terms of providing value to its shareholders. But General Electric had a negative economic profit of $304 million, which implies that the firm's management was losing value.[18] This apparent contradiction between economic profit and market value added may be because of the fact that economic profit, although theoretically forward looking, is based on historical, single-period accounting data and market value added is based on forward-looking stock prices.[19] Therefore, Equation 3.7 is nonsensical in the case in which there is an economic loss and a positive market value added.

Challenges in Applying Value-Added Measures

Even advocates of economic profit do not prescribe a particular formula for its calculation. Each firm is an individual case; the adjustments to arrive at operating profits after taxes are different for each firm. Therefore, from the perspective of the financial analyst who must rely on financial statements and other publicly available information to determine economic profit, applying EVA measures is difficult. Although a formula could be developed to deal with the most common adjustments, exceptions to the general rules, which must be dealt with, will always exist.

Economic profit has ambiguous elements, most notably adjustments to operating income and cost of capital.[20] These ambiguous elements result in several major problems when applying economic profit. First, two analysts may apply different formulas and draw different conclusions regarding a firm's relative performance.[21] Second, when applied internally to reward management, economic profit is subject to potential manipulation. Unfortunately, manipulation is the problem that economic profit was developed to solve—avoiding misleading accounting measurements.[22]

Another problem with economic profit is how the cost of capital is calculated:

- *The use of the CAPM.* Most applications of economic profit use a CAPM-based cost of equity. The CAPM has been challenged, however, as inadequately capturing the risk–return relationship.[23]
- *The estimate of the market risk premium.* In the applications prescribed by Stewart (1991), a risk premium of 6 percent is used, which contrasts with the lower

---

[18]See Walbert (1993, p. 65). Other conflicts in the top 10 MVA firms for 1992 include AT&T (MVA rank of 7), Exxon Corporation (MVA rank of 11), and Pfizer (MVA rank of 17)—all of which had negative EVA values.

[19]As previously shown, slight differences in the estimated cost of capital can result in quite different conclusions regarding economic profit and, hence, performance.

[20]These ambiguous elements are not the fault of economic profit, per se, but the starting point of the calculations: reported financial statements prepared according to generally accepted accounting principles.

[21]Stewart (1994) discusses the customization of EVA calculations for particular companies and applications.

[22]See Brossy and Balkcom (1994) and "Stern Stewart EVA Roundtable" (1994, p. 66).

[23]See, for example, Fama and French (1992) and Haugen (1995) for a discussion of the challenges to the CAPM.

risk premium of 5 percent used by Copeland, Koller, and Murrin (1994). Does it matter? Using the 6 percent risk premium produces a cost of capital for Hershey of 9.53 percent (instead of 8.86 percent) and a lower economic profit.[24]

* *The use of historical data.* Some methods of calculating the WACC use historical-based data for the cost of capital instead of the marginal cost. Using historical data is reflected in three aspects of the cost-of-capital calculation: the use of a historical beta, the use of averages of historical capital structure proportions, and the use of current yields on long-term debt (as opposed to expected yields). The estimated cost of capital is sensitive to the choice of data.

Whether these issues affect the assessment of performance and relative performance is, of course, an empirical issue.

HOLT's CFROI

To evaluate firm performance, an alternative to economic profit is a return-on-investment measure known as the HOLT method.[25] This measure, referred to as CFROI, is an IRR measure but not in the traditional sense. The key difference between CFROI and the IRR typically seen in capital budgeting is that cash flows and investments are stated in constant monetary units in CFROI, which overcomes a deficiency of the traditional return on investment measures.

CFROI and other cash-focused measures are a promising approach to performance measurement.[26] CFROI is, in essence, a rate of return. But as with other rate-of-return measures, high CFROIs are neither good nor bad because the return on an investment, to be attractive, should compensate the investor for the investment's risk. Therefore, when using a return measure such as CFROI, a benchmark is also needed that reflects the amount of risk—the firm's cost of capital.

CFROI Calculations. Basically six steps are involved in calculating a firm's CFROI:

Step 1: Calculate the life of the assets.
Step 2: Calculate gross cash flow.
Step 3: Calculate gross cash investment.
Step 4: Calculate the sum of nondepreciating assets.
Step 5: Solve for the rate of return (CFROI).
Step 6: Compare CFROI with the benchmark.

CFROI is the return on investment expected over the average life of the firm's existing assets. The basic idea is that the firm has made current and past investment decisions that are expected to generate future cash flows, and CFROI is a measure of the return on those investments. The gross cash flow (Step 2) is the estimate of the cash flow expected each year over the life of the assets. Gross cash flow is based on the current year's income adjusted for noncash operating expenses and financing expenses. The gross cash investment (Step 3) represents the gross invested capital in the firm in the current year. The nondepreciating assets (Step 4) represent the terminal value of the firm at the end of the average life of the firm's

---

[24]Ranking firms according to economic profit should not be affected significantly by the choice of the risk premium as long as the firms' betas are close to 1. But in those cases with betas much different from 1, the choice of the risk premium begins to affect firms' relative rankings.

[25]Two firms use the HOLT method in their consulting practice: HOLT Value Associates, LP (dealing primarily with portfolio management) and BCG/HOLT (dealing primarily with corporate management). Slight differences arise in the calculation of CFROIs by these two firms.

[26]See Reimann (1988) and Birchard (1994) for a discussion of the benefits from these measures.

existing assets. CFROI is thus the return that equates the gross investment (the present value) with the sum of the present value of expected annual cash flows and the present value of the terminal value. The basic calculations in determining the CFROI will be demonstrated, as previously, using Hershey.

■ *Asset life*. The average life of the firm's assets is used as the analysis horizon in calculating the CFROI. Determining precisely the average life of the firm's assets-in-place would be difficult, so an approximation is necessary. One approximation is the median of the ratio of the gross plant assets divided by the depreciation expense for the current year and each of the two previous years. To see how this works, look at Hershey for each year during the period 1991 through 1993:

	1993 (millions)	1992 (millions)	1991 (millions)
Gross plant assets	$2,041.764	$1,797.437	$1,581.296
Less: Construction in progress	(171.100)	(196.900)	(170.500)
Less: Land	(48.239)	(40.163)	(37.911)
Depreciable gross assets	$1,822.425	$1,560.374	$1,372.885
Divided by: Depreciation expense	100.124	84.434	72.735
Estimated asset life (years)	18.202	18.480	18.875

The median of the three years' estimated asset life is 18.48 years. Because working with whole years is easier than working with partial years, assume that the horizon for the analysis is 18 years.

■ *Gross cash flow*. The gross cash flow is calculated by starting with net income after taxes and then adding back noncash operating expenses and financing expenses deducted to arrive at net income. Using 1993 Hershey data results in the following calculation of gross cash flow:

	Amount (millions)
Net income after tax but before extraordinary items	$297.233
Add: Depreciation and amortization	100.124
Add: Interest expense	34.870
Add: Operating rental expense	24.524
Add: Deferred taxes	11.047
Less: Special item	(80.642)
Add: Tax benefit from special item	40.000
Gross cash flow	$427.156

Three primary differences exist between the gross cash flow used in this analysis and the adjusted operating profits used to calculate economic profits. First, goodwill amortization is added back to net income in the calculation of economic profit, whereas both depreciation and amortization are added back to arrive at gross cash flow, which is a fundamental difference between the two approaches. In determining economic profit, depreciation is not added back because it is considered a cost of the business; that is, depreciation represents the use of the assets. In determining the CFROI's gross cash flow, the objective is to reflect cash flows; hence, depreciation is added to income to reflect actual cash flows.[27] The second difference between the two

---

[27]Another rationale for adding back depreciation is that the depreciation expense reflects an element that can be easily manipulated by the judicious choice of depreciation methods. Adding back the depreciation expense results in more comparable returns among firms.

methods is that in the determination of economic profits, the tax expense is adjusted to reflect actual cash taxes. No such adjustment is made in determining the CFROI's gross cash flow. Third, operating rental expenses are added back to determine gross cash flow for CFROI, whereas only the estimated interest portion of rentals is added back to reflect economic profit.

■ *Gross cash investment.* Gross cash investment consists of book assets grossed up for accumulated depreciation and the value of operating leases not presented in financial statements.

	Amount (millions)
Gross plant, property, and equipment	$2,041.764
Add: Present value of operating leases	337.291
Add: Goodwill	473.408
Add: Accumulated goodwill amortization	73.400
Gross cash investment	$2,925.863

The calculation here of the value of operating leases is different from that used for economic profit. The future operating lease commitments are discounted over a period that reflects the life of the assets—18 years in the case of Hershey. The present value of the operating leases is calculated as a stream of current rental expense for noncancelable leases discounted at the real rate of interest on the firm's debt. The rental expense for 1993 is $24.524 million (footnote 13). Assuming that the real debt rate is, say, 3 percent, the present value of the operating leases is $337.291 million.

Keep in mind that when determining economic profit, gross cash investment for CFROI and invested capital differ in several respects. One difference is that accumulated goodwill is added back into invested capital.[28] Another difference is that assets are grossed up for accumulated depreciation for CFROI, but only the amount net of depreciation is figured into invested capital for economic profit purposes.

■ *Nondepreciating assets.* The terminal value consists of the expected nondepreciating assets of the firm, which includes land, net working capital, and any investments in marketable securities. For Hershey, the terminal value is

	Amount (millions)
Land	$ 48.239
Add: Net working capital	442.946
Add: Other assets	31.783
Terminal value	$522.968

■ *Caveats.* One of the key elements in CFROI that is not reflected in these calculations is the adjustment of the financial items to reflect current dollars, which requires the following adjustments:

- a monetary inflation adjustment to gross cash flow to reflect monetary gains and losses;
- a current-dollar investment adjustment to gross investment to reflect the current-dollar values of prior periods' capital expenditures; and
- an inflation adjustment for land to adjust the terminal value such that the value of land is in current-dollar amounts.

In practice, these adjustments involve calculations that are of a proprietary nature and,

[28]In some applications, accumulated goodwill is added back into the CFROI's invested capital.

©The Research Foundation of the ICFA

therefore, are not presented here.[29]

■ *CFROI.* CFROI is the return that equates the gross cash investment with the sum of the present value of the annual gross cash flow (assumed constant each year over the life of the assets) and the present value of the terminal value.[30] In the case of Hershey,

Gross cash investment	= $2,925.863 million
Gross cash flow	= $ 427.156 million
Nondepreciating assets	= $ 522.968 million
Asset life	= 18 years

CFROI, using the above amounts, is 13.310 percent.[31] Keep in mind that this rate is in nominal terms; that is, these values have not been translated into current dollars.[32] Once the adjustments to current-dollar terms are made, CFROI (which is, in effect, an IRR) is then compared with a benchmark return. Given the cost of capital that was calculated earlier in this chapter, one can see that Hershey has a nominal CFROI that exceeds its nominal cost of capital.

■ *Discussion.* The CFROI approach does not lend itself well to simplified examples because several of the calculations are proprietary in nature, but this type of approach is attractive for a number of reasons:

- CFROI provides an assessment of performance in the familiar return-on-investment terms instead of in dollar terms (as is the case of economic profit).
- The CFROI return calculation overcomes some of the drawbacks of using a traditional return-on-investment approach because the return is stated in real (instead of nominal) terms, thereby facilitating comparisons across time and across borders.
- In the CFROI approach, accounting income is translated into cash flows, which is a better reflection of performance. Using cash flows improves on traditional measures and involves adjustments that are similar (yet not identical) to those made to accounting data in calculating economic profit.

A more detailed description of CFROI can be found in Thomas and Edwards (1993) and Madden (1995).

One drawback to using CFROI is that the end result of the calculations is in current-dollar terms. In the Hershey example, CFROI based on readily available information is approximately 12 percent, but CFROI requires making current-dollar adjustments, which results in a return on investment that relies on the quality of these current-dollar adjustments. Small differences in the current-dollar adjustments, which require esti-

---

[29]Bartley Madden, a partner of HOLT Value Associates, kindly provided rough estimates of these adjustments for Hershey's 1993 calculations. The estimate of the current-dollar adjustments to nondepreciating assets is $74 million, and the estimate of the current-dollar adjustments to gross cash investments is $624 million.

[30]In time-value-of-money vernacular, the present value is the gross cash investment, the periodic cash flow (the payment) is the gross cash flow, the future value is the terminal value, and the asset life is the number of periods.

[31]The calculation of CFROI is straightforward when it is the rate that equates the gross cash investment to the future gross cash flow stream and the nondepreciating assets (the terminal value). Therefore, using time-value-of-money terms, future value = $522.968 million, present value = $2,925.863 million, payment = $427.156 million, and number of periods = 18.

[32]Using the estimates of the current-dollar adjustments provided by HOLT Value Associates, CFROI for Hershey is 10.254 percent, which still exceeds Hershey's cost of capital. This value for CFROI has not, by the way, been translated into real terms. It should be noted, however, that HOLT Value Associates calculates an inflation-adjusted benchmark discount rate by using methods that differ from the traditional cost-of-capital calculations.

mates of the current value of inventories, plant and equipment, and land, can result in different CFROI values. If the current-dollar adjustment for inventories were $400 million, gross plant $700 million, and land $50 million, CFROI would be 10.2 percent. If, instead, the current-dollar adjustments were $300 million, $800 million, and $0, respectively, CFROI would be 9.7 percent. Therefore, CFROI is sensitive to the current-dollar adjustments.

Another drawback is that CFROI is difficult to translate into an evaluation of performance. Is a CFROI of 10 percent good or bad? The answer lies in the comparison of the CFROI with a benchmark return, which should reflect the risk associated with the firm's capital investment. Consistent with the CFROI approach, this benchmark should be a discount rate that is stated in real terms. Instead of the traditional (and familiar) cost of capital that uses readily available market data in its estimate, the benchmark for CFROI requires using a cost of capital stated in real instead of nominal terms. This adjustment adds one more layer of estimation in the calculation of the cost of capital.

Summary

The increased attention to performance measurement for compensation purposes has led to measures that appear to be an improvement on traditional measures. Leading the charge has been Stern Stewart's advocation of the use of economic profit to measure performance. Although not a new concept, the application of economic profit to evaluate performance has focused attention on refining these measures.

In this chapter, we applied economic profit, market value added, and CFROI to Hershey for 1993. Our estimates show that Hershey's management added value according to economic profit and market value added. Our estimate of CFROI confirms that Hershey's management added value.

The concepts of economic profit and market value added are appealing because they provide measures of performance that are consistent with financial theories, but our examples point out some of the potential problems with using these measures. First, the estimate of economic profit requires many adjustments to accounting data to remove distortions attributed to accounting methods. Some of the data needed to make these adjustments are not readily available in published financial statements. Second, the estimate of economic profit is sensitive to the estimated cost of capital; small changes in the cost of capital can result in large changes in estimated economic profit. And last, conflicts may arise between economic profit and market value added. These conflicts arise, in part, from the two different approaches to assessing value added: Estimating economic profit requires using accounting data to estimate value added, whereas estimating market value added requires using the market's assessment of value.

An alternative measure of performance, CFROI, is a return on investment that adjusts for inflation, hence making the performance measure comparable across time and borders. Like economic profit, CFROI is sensitive to the elements in the calculations—in particular, the current-dollar adjustments and the selection of the real cost of capital.

Despite the potential sensitivity of these measures of performance to elements in their calculation, these performance measures are useful in examining changes in the firm's performance year to year. In this case, the key is to be consistent in the calculations from year to year. For example, if the same method of adjusting to current dollars is applied to calculate CFROI every year, then focusing on how CFROI changes from one year to the next mitigates the concern over its sensitivity to the adjustments.

Perhaps the greatest benefit from the value added and CFROI measures is their ability to shift the focus away from accounting profits and toward measures that more closely represent true economic performance. The measures' developers face challenges in devising methods that both remove accounting distortions from reported financial data and capture the true costs of capital, but the discussion and debate surrounding these measures will help refine them to better represent a firm's performance.

4. Comparison of Alternative Performance Measures

The ultimate test of a measure of performance for a publicly traded firm is its stock price—the market's collective judgment of the value of the company's ownership interests. Therefore, our evaluation uses market performance measures as a benchmark.[1] We believe that the goal of a firm's management should be to maximize shareholder wealth. To that end, the performance of any firm should be judged using some type of share price performance measures. In this chapter, we compare both the traditional and recently developed value-added measures with share price performance to gauge how well these measures reflect the market's assessment of performance.[2] We cannot directly test how well these measures assess the performance of a particular division, product line, or manager, but we can examine how these measures assess the performance of a firm compared with market measures of performance, thus providing information on their usefulness.

The Sample

The empirical comparisons require stock price and financial statement data. Financial statement data are taken from Standard & Poor's Compustat, and stock price data are taken from the University of Chicago's Center for Research in Security Prices (CRSP) databases. Several sample years are selected to examine the robustness of these measures for different market and economic environments. We chose five sample years, 1988 through 1992.

The sample contains companies that satisfy the following criteria:

1. The company's common stock traded on the New York Stock Exchange during the sample years.
2. The company is not in a financial or public utility line of business, based on Standard Industrial Classification codes.
3. Monthly stock price data for the company are available in CRSP's databases for the sample years.
4. Financial statement information is available for the company from Compustat's annual industrial and research databases for the sample years.[3]
5. The company's fiscal year end is in December.

The first criterion allows for the comparison of our findings with published exam-

---

[1]Because the market-value-added measure includes the change in market value, we expect to find that market value added is closely related to the market performance benchmarks.

[2]The CFROI measure is not examined in this empirical study because the key adjustments for current-dollar translations are proprietary.

[3]We include firms that are listed in the Compustat Research database and firms in the Annual Industrial database to avoid a survivorship bias. For a discussion of the potential problems with survivorship bias, see Hagin (1988) and Ross (1994).

ples, thus providing confidence in our results. The second criterion is necessary because several of the measures are not applicable to financial or utility companies.[4] The third criterion allows for the calculation of the share price benchmarks. The fourth criterion allows for the calculation of the traditional and recently developed performance measures. Because several of the performance measures require detailed financial statement data, we perform the analysis for a different number of firms each year based on availability of data. The last criterion permits comparisons of performance among firms within a given sample year.[5] The resultant sample sizes, noted in Table 4.1, range from a low of 259 firms for 1989 to 282 firms for 1992.

Table 4.1. Average Benchmark Returns for Each Year, 1988–92

Year	Number of Securities in Sample	Total Stock Return	Market Model-Adjusted Return	Size-Adjusted Return
1988	262	13.5%	–5.3%	–2.4%
1989	259	15.9	3.8	3.6
1990	267	8.8	5.5	–1.5
1991	274	15.3	–8.0	–0.4
1992	282	18.5	–0.9	2.2

Problems arise in coordinating financial statement data and market data. Suppose we want to evaluate IBM Corporation's financial performance for 1990 by comparing the return on assets with the common stock's total return. Return on assets for 1990 uses income statement and balance sheet data for the fiscal year 1990, which happens to be the calendar year. If we compare the 1990 return on assets with the common stock's total return for calendar year 1990, the results will be out of sync because the stock's return is measured over a period in which some of the 1990 financial data are not available. Because financial statements must be released soon after the fiscal year end, we allow three months for this information to be reflected in the stock's price.[6]

The Variables

The comparison of measures of performance requires us to calculate three types of variables. The first is the benchmark variable that is based on a firm's common stock market performance. The benchmark variables represent the market's measure of performance. The second type is the traditional performance variable, as discussed in Chapter 2. The traditional performance measures represent widely used measures of performance. The third type is the value-added measure, discussed in Chapter 3. These variables are estimates of value added, based on economic profit and market value added.

Benchmarks. We develop three benchmarks to use in our analysis. The first is the simplest: the *annual or total stock return* (TSR). This return is calculated by compound-

[4]The value-added measures are not applicable to financial service firms because the definition of capital is quite different for these firms. The value-added measures are not applicable to public utility firms because these firms are regulated in such a way as to produce a specific return on capital.

[5]Some of the published rankings of firms based on return and value added (see, for example, Tully [1993]) do not distinguish among firms based on fiscal year end, which causes a mismatch of the data among firms and with any market return data.

[6]This approach is similar to that used by Fama and French (1992) and others in studies that use both financial statement data and market data. The purpose of this strategy is to avoid look-ahead bias. Therefore, when we report stock performance for the sample year 1990, for example, we are reporting performance for April 1, 1990, through March 31, 1991, a period that we assume captures the financial information released for the fiscal year 1990.

ing monthly returns for the stock over the year, April 1 of the sample year through March 31 of the following year. We include this measure not only because it is simple but also because it allows comparisons with published performance of some of the recent measures.

The second benchmark is a market model-adjusted measure. This expected return is based on parameters from a market model estimated over the 60 monthly returns prior to April 1 of the sample year. The market model regression is used to estimate the intercept and slope coefficients, which are then used to generate expected returns for each month in the sample year. We then calculate the security's annual return by compounding the monthly returns and calculate the expected annual stock return by compounding the monthly expected returns. The difference between the security's actual annual stock return and the expected annual return is the excess return, or the *market model-adjusted return* (MAR).

The third benchmark is a *size-adjusted return* (SAR). This return is calculated by first placing each security into a decile based on the size of the equity's market value as of March 31 of the sample year. The size deciles are formed by ranking all NYSE firms by their market value of equity on March 31 of each year. The average return for each size decile is calculated for each month in the sample year by equally weighting each security in the decile. For a given security, its SAR is the difference between its total annual stock return and the total annual stock return for the size decile for which it is a member, where each annual return is calculated by compounding the corresponding monthly returns.[7]

These three benchmarks form a basis for comparing each performance measure that is based on financial statement data. Descriptive statistics for each benchmark are presented in Table 4.1. The excess returns, MAR and SAR, are close to zero, as expected.

We calculate correlations between the benchmarks to see how closely they rate the performance of the firms. We present both parametric and nonparametric correlations (and related tests of significance) in Table 4.2 for each sample year.[8] The returns for the three benchmarks are highly correlated with one another, with the closest relation being between total stock returns and size-adjusted returns. In other words, the benchmarks produce similar rankings of the stocks' performance.

Table 4.2. Parametric and Nonparametric Correlations among Benchmark Returns for Each Year, 1988–92

	TSRs and MARs		TSRs and SARs	
Year	Pearson Correlation Coefficient (parametric)	Spearman Correlation Coefficient (nonparametric)	Pearson Correlation Coefficient (parametric)	Spearman Correlation Coefficient (nonparametric)
1988	0.93	0.85	0.99	0.98
1989	0.91	0.91	0.94	0.94
1990	0.92	0.89	0.99	0.99
1991	0.90	0.86	0.98	0.96
1992	0.91	0.90	0.98	0.98

Note: All correlation coefficients are different from zero at the 5 percent level of significance.

---

[7]We follow a methodology similar to that used in Lakonishok, Shleifer, and Vishny (1994).

[8]The nonparametric correlations are similar to the more familiar parametric correlations. The nonparametric, or Spearman, correlations involve first ranking the sample cases by each of two variables (in this case, two of the return benchmarks) and then testing whether the rankings are similar.

Traditional Measures of Performance. We look at five traditional measures of performance:

- basic earning power, defined as the ratio of operating earnings to total assets;
- return on assets, defined as the ratio of net income to total assets;
- return on equity, defined as the ratio of net income to the book value of equity;
- cash flow return on assets; and
- Tobin's q proxy, defined as the ratio of two sums: The numerator is the sum of the book value of debt, the liquidating value of preferred stock, and the market value of common stock; the denominator is the sum of the book value of equity, the book value of preferred stock, and the book value of debt, the sum of which is total assets.

Each measure is calculated for each firm and each sample year. We present descriptive statistics for each of the traditional measures for each year in Table 4.3. Correlation coefficients between each of the traditional measures for a representative year, 1990, are presented in Table 4.4. We present only one year of correlations to keep the presentation simple, although the correlations are similar for each of the sample years. Each of the pairwise correlations shown in Table 4.4 is different from zero at the 5 percent level of significance, which indicates that the traditional measures provide similar evaluations of performance.

Table 4.3. Descriptive Statistics of Traditional Performance Measures

Year	Basic Earning Power	Return on Assets	Return on Equity	Cash Flow Return on Assets	Tobin's q Proxy
1988	0.10	0.06	0.20	0.11	1.42
	(0.05)	(0.04)	(0.26)	(0.05)	(0.50)
1989	0.11	0.06	0.14	0.10	1.45
	(0.05)	(0.04)	(0.31)	(0.05)	(0.56)
1990	0.09	0.05	0.18	0.10	1.49
	(0.05)	(0.04)	(1.11)	(0.05)	(0.69)
1991	0.09	0.04	0.16	0.09	1.57
	(0.06)	(0.05)	(2.18)	(0.06)	(0.78)
1992	0.09	0.04	0.11	0.09	1.64
	(0.06)	(0.05)	(0.72)	(0.05)	(0.69)

Note: Table values are averages, with standard deviations in parentheses.

Table 4.4. Correlations between Traditional Performance Measures, 1990

	Return on Assets	Return on Equity	Cash Flow Return on Assets	Tobin's q Proxy
Basic earning power	0.87	0.21	0.78	0.76
Return on assets		0.18	0.84	0.75
Return on equity			0.15	0.18
Cash flow return on assets				0.67

Note: Table values are parametric correlations. All correlation coefficients are different from zero at the 5 percent level of significance.

Value-Added Measures of Performance. Several value-added measures are calculated to assess a firm's performance. The first is economic profit, which is the difference between the net operating profit after tax (NOPAT) and the cost of capital, stated in dollar terms. Firms are ranked by the amount of economic profit that is generated in a period. Economic profit is defined in Equation 3.1 and is calculated here in the manner described in Chapter 3.[9,10]

Economic profit is the dollar amount of value added during a period. By construction, economic profit is affected by a firm's size (that is, its capital); larger firms, with greater amounts of capital to use, will generate a disproportionate amount of economic profit. Therefore, we create a second measure of performance that is similar to the traditional form of a return but with refinements in the calculations of the benefit from using capital and the amount of capital. We divide NOPAT by average invested capital (that is, the average of the beginning of the year's capital and the end of the year's capital) to produce the return on capital.[11] Because we are dividing NOPAT by capital, the cost of capital does not affect this return.

To facilitate comparison of firms, we also develop a proxy that is a variation on economic profit.[12] This measure is the spread between the return on capital (that is, NOPAT divided by invested capital) and the cost of capital (expressed in percentage terms). When multiplied by invested capital, this spread produces the dollar economic profit. This measure is expressed in Equation 3.7. The difference between the return on capital and the spread is the cost of capital.

The fourth value-added proxy is the change in the market value added. Market value added is defined in Equation 3.6, and its change is calculated as described in Chapter 3— the sum of the change in the market value of equity and the change in the book value of debt and preferred stock. This measure may be sensitive to the size of the firm, however, because firms with large capital bases can more easily generate greater amounts of value added. Therefore, for standardization we create a fifth proxy, the percentage of change in market value added (i.e., market value added divided by beginning total capital).[13]

We provide descriptive statistics for each of the value-added measures in Table 4.5. Economic profit and the change in market value are both represented in dollar terms. Notice that in four of the five years, the average economic profit is negative, but the average is not significantly different from zero at the 5 percent level.[14] We provide correlations between each of the value-added measures for 1990 in Table

---

[9]One difference, however, between economic profit in the empirical study and that described in Chapter 3 is that rentals beyond the fifth year are not available for most firms, so this element is left out in the empirical study; in other words, the present value of operating leases is the present value of the reported next five years' rentals.

[10]In estimating the cost of capital for each firm, we use the following assumptions and proxies: (1) The risk-free rate is proxied by the U.S. Treasury 10-year bond rate; (2) the long-term debt interest rate is assumed to be the prevailing yield on similar-rated debt; (3) the preferred stock yield is proxied by the average yield on seasoned preferred stock issues; (4) the common stock beta is calculated using the monthly returns for the 60 months prior to March 31 of the sample year; and (5) the risk premium for the market is 5 percent. All debt and preferred stock yields are from Moody's Investors Service's *Industrial Manual*, 1989 to 1993. The average cost of capital ranges from a low of 8.12 percent in 1992 to a high of 10.12 percent in 1988.

[11]We use the average of the beginning-of-the-year and end-of-the-year capital in our calculations of economic profit and market value added. This technique differs from Stewart's approach (1991, p. 173); he uses beginning-of-the-year capital to estimate economic profit and end-of-the-year capital to estimate market value added.

[12]The need to standardize among firms is recognized by Stewart (1991, p. 167). If comparisons are made among years, further standardization is needed.

[13]The need to standardize the change in market value added is recognized by Stewart (1991, p. 173), with further standardization required if comparisons are made over time. Despite the recognized need to standardize, many published rankings of firms do not use standardization.

[14]We examined firms with extreme negative values of economic profit. These firms were, in general, fairly large and were experiencing flat or declining earnings. For example, in 1989, the five largest negative values of economic profit were for Ford Motor Company, Chevron Corporation, Occidental Petroleum, Xerox Corporation, and McDonnell Douglas Corporation.

4.6. In all years, the percentage of change in market value added is not correlated with the other measures, although significant correlations exist between each of these other measures.

Table 4.5. Descriptive Statistics of Value-Added Performance Measures

Year	Economic Profit	Return on Capital	Spread between Return on Capital and Cost of Capital	Change in Market Value Added	Percentage of Change in Market Value Added
1988	−$28.46	0.10	−0.002	$833.33	0.19
	($319.87)	(0.07)	(0.06)	($572.03)	(1.56)
1989	−3.88	0.10	−0.001	669.36	0.22
	(464.28)	(0.06)	(0.05)	(1,982.57)	(1.23)
1990	−41.28	0.09	−0.003	478.40	−0.05
	(650.06)	(0.06)	(0.06)	(2,692.00)	(2.20)
1991	−43.64	0.09	−0.001	545.66	0.01
	(882.30)	(0.07)	(0.07)	(2,234.29)	(2.76)
1992	9.95	0.10	0.014	442.25	−0.10
	(715.19)	(0.08)	(0.08)	(2,386.18)	(4.18)

Note: Table values are averages, with standard deviations in parentheses.

Table 4.6. Correlations between Value-Added Performance Measures, 1990

	Return on Capital	Spread between Return on Capital and Cost of Capital	Change in Market Value Added	Percentage Change in Market Value Added
Economic profit	0.39*	0.39*	0.42*	0.04
Return on capital		0.95*	0.42*	0.07
Spread between return on capital and cost of capital			0.45*	0.09
Change in market value added				0.06

*Indicates a correlation coefficient different from zero at the 5 percent level of significance.

Note: Table values are parametric correlations.

Empirical Results

The focus of the analysis is on how well the traditional and value-added measures of performance correspond to the benchmarks that are based on market performance. Each performance measure is compared with the benchmarks using both parametric correlations and nonparametric correlations.

Traditional Measures. Before we examine how well the value-added measures rate firms relative to the benchmarks, we look at how well the simpler, traditional methods of performance measurement rate firms. The parametric and nonparametric correlations between the five traditional measures and the benchmark returns for each year are reported in Table 4.7. Correlations that are different from zero at the 5 percent level of significance are noted. Based on the method of constructing each of these measures, we expect a positive correlation with stock returns, which, in general, is what we find. Furthermore, the parametric correlations with the returns are not as strong as

Table 4.7. Correlations between the Traditional Performance Measures and Stock Returns, 1988–92

Traditional Performance Measure	Year	TSRs		MARs		SARs	
		Pearson Correlation Coefficient (parametric)	Spearman Correlation Coefficient (nonparametric)	Pearson Correlation Coefficient (parametric)	Spearman Correlation Coefficient (nonparametric)	Pearson Correlation Coefficient (parametric)	Spearman Correlation Coefficient (nonparametric)
Basic earning power	1988	0.01	0.05	-0.11	-0.11	-0.03	0.00
	1989	0.21*	0.19*	0.06	0.09	0.13*	0.11
	1990	0.42*	0.46*	0.21*	0.26*	0.37*	0.41*
	1991	0.20*	0.20*	0.04	0.03	0.27*	0.27*
	1992	-0.06	-0.02	-0.23*	-0.20*	-0.05	-0.22*
Return on assets	1988	0.00	0.01	-0.11	-0.13	-0.02	-0.02
	1989	0.23*	0.19*	0.11	0.11	0.15*	0.12*
	1990	0.43*	0.45*	0.24*	0.27*	0.40*	0.41*
	1991	0.12*	0.16*	0.02	0.00	0.18*	0.22*
	1992	-0.01	0.06	-0.17*	-0.11	0.01	0.07
Return on equity	1988	0.15*	0.13*	0.11*	-0.01	0.14*	0.09
	1989	0.04	0.15*	0.00	0.06	0.01	0.07
	1990	0.13*	0.40*	0.06	0.23*	0.12*	0.36*
	1991	-0.06	0.14*	0.01	0.00	-0.07	0.18*
	1992	-0.03	0.04	-0.04	-0.08	-0.04	0.04
Cash flow return on assets	1988	0.04	0.06	-0.04	-0.05	0.02	0.02
	1989	0.09	0.18*	0.19*	0.13*	0.10	0.09
	1990	0.31*	0.30*	0.15*	0.16*	0.27*	0.25*
	1991	0.08	0.09	-0.02	-0.09	0.14*	0.16*
	1992	0.04	0.06	-0.11	-0.09	0.06	0.08
Tobin's q proxy	1988	0.13*	0.10	0.01	-0.02	0.10	0.07
	1989	0.27*	0.31*	0.12	0.18*	0.16*	0.20*
	1990	0.45*	0.40*	0.29*	0.24*	0.41*	0.36*
	1991	0.16*	0.16*	-0.06	-0.10	0.23*	0.24*
	1992	0.00	0.05	-0.20*	-0.15*	0.00	0.04

*Indicates that the correlation coefficient is different from zero at the 5 percent level of significance.

the rank correlations.

No one measure dominates in terms of the correlation with stock returns, although the basic earning power ratio, the return on assets, and Tobin's q are more highly correlated with stock returns than return on equity and cash flow return on assets. For both 1988 and 1992, the relation between these measures and stock returns is weak.

Value-Added Measures. The parametric and nonparametric correlations between each of the five value-added measures and stock returns are presented in Table 4.8 for each year. A positive relation exists in most years. Similar to the results with the traditional measures, the results for 1988 and 1992 are quite different from those for the three intervening years, especially for economic value added.

The use of the dollar amount of economic profit as a performance measure bears little relation to stock returns, as indicated by the majority of insignificant correlations and the presence of significant negative correlations in 1992. Only in 1990 do consistently positive significant correlations exist between economic profit and stock returns. The return on capital (NOPAT divided by invested capital) is positively correlated with stock returns in 1989, 1990, and 1991. Thus, there is improvement relative to the dollar amount of economic profit. Negative correlations exist in 1992, however, and little relation is found between the spread and returns in 1988. Interestingly, removing the cost of capital does not improve the correlations with stock returns, which can be seen by comparing the correlations for return on capital with those of the spread in Table 4.8. The correlations of the spread with stock returns are not much different from those for the return on capital with stock returns.[15]

The market-value-added measures are statistically significantly correlated with stock returns. This association is attributed to the use of the change in market values directly in the measure. The change in market value is significantly correlated with stock returns in terms of the rankings, as is the percentage of change in market value added. Market value added and stock returns are not perfectly correlated, however, because the market-value-added measure includes the change in the book value of debt and preferred stock, whereas the stock returns do not. Therefore, market-value-added measures should be used with caution unless care is taken (1) to determine the market values of debt and preferred stock and (2) to include these values in the estimate of market value added.

Market-value-added measures may not be perfectly correlated with market-adjusted and size-adjusted stock returns for another reason: The market-value-added measures do not control for general market movements and risk. The market value of a stock may increase because of correct, value-maximizing decisions by management, but the market value of a stock may also increase because stocks in general are increasing in value or because the stock has a different risk from the market. Looking at the market-value-added measures and stock returns, therefore, does not give a complete picture. Table 4.8 shows that the market-value-added measures are highly correlated with both market-adjusted and size-adjusted returns, suggesting that the controls for market movements, at least in the sample years 1988 through 1992, are not crucial.

The results with respect to market-value-added measures indicate that these measures are good but not perfect proxies for the performance of the firm's management over a period of time. Unlike economic profit, the application of market-value-added measures is limited to assessing the performance of the firm as a whole and cannot be

---

[15]We also calculated economic profit, return on capital, and the spread based on ending capital with nearly identical results.

©The Research Foundation of the ICFA

Table 4.8. Correlations between Value-Added Measures of Performance and Stock Returns, 1988–92

Valued-Added Performance Measure	Year	TSRs		MARs		SARs	
		Pearson Correlation Coefficient (parametric)	Spearman Correlation Coefficient (nonparametric)	Pearson Correlation Coefficient (parametric)	Spearman Correlation Coefficient (nonparametric)	Pearson Correlation Coefficient (parametric)	Spearman Correlation Coefficient (nonparametric)
Economic profit	1988	0.02	0.07	-0.03	-0.04	0.02	0.05
	1989	0.11	0.10	0.07	0.00	0.08	0.05
	1990	0.26*	0.40*	0.23*	0.25*	0.27*	0.39
	1991	0.02	0.08	-0.03	-0.04	0.03	0.12*
	1992	-0.15	-0.12*	-0.20*	-0.21*	0.02	-0.10
Return on capital	1988	0.01	0.08	-0.09	-0.04	-0.03	0.05
	1989	0.16*	0.15*	0.03	0.06	0.06	0.06
	1990	0.41*	0.37*	0.24*	0.18	0.37*	0.33*
	1991	0.14*	0.16*	-0.01	0.00	0.21*	0.24*
	1992	-0.16*	-0.11	-0.29*	-0.26*	-0.14*	-0.11
Spread between return on capital and cost of capital	1988	-0.02	0.10	-0.08	-0.04	-0.01	0.06
	1989	0.17*	0.19*	-0.01	0.06	0.07	0.07
	1990	0.42*	0.40*	0.23*	0.21*	0.37*	0.35*
	1991	0.09	0.10	-0.03	-0.01	0.16*	0.16*
	1992	-0.15*	-0.09	-0.26*	-0.21*	-0.13*	-0.09
Change in market value added	1988	0.11	0.61*	0.06	0.54*	0.10	0.59*
	1989	0.36*	0.65*	0.28*	0.58*	0.21	0.55*
	1990	0.50*	0.73*	0.42*	0.69*	0.47*	0.73*
	1991	0.33*	0.64*	0.23*	0.46*	0.37*	0.69*
	1992	0.36*	0.57*	0.32*	0.49*	0.38*	0.57*
Percentage of change in market value added	1988	0.18*	0.48*	0.15*	0.42*	0.17*	0.47*
	1989	0.33*	0.65*	0.28*	0.58*	0.31*	0.61*
	1990	-0.03	0.63*	-0.07	0.58*	-0.03	0.63*
	1991	0.07	0.65*	0.04	0.54*	0.10	0.63*
	1992	0.14*	0.63*	0.14	0.57	0.15*	0.62*

*Indicates that the correlation coefficient is different from zero at the 5 percent level of significance.

used to assess performance of a division or other subset of the firm's management. As measures of the performance of the firm as a whole, however, market-adjusted and size-adjusted stock returns are reasonable alternatives to using the market-value-added measures.

As mentioned previously, the ranking of firms on the basis of economic value added and market value added may be affected by the size of the firm.[16] We examine the relation between size and economic profit and market-value measures of performance to see the extent to which rankings by these measures are affected by a firm's size. To illustrate this point, we represent size two ways: the book value of equity and total assets, where both values are measured at the beginning of the period. The relations between size and economic profit and the relation between size and market value added (both in dollar values) are shown in Table 4.9. The correlations between the absolute values of these two measures and the two measures of size (beginning book value of equity and total assets) are positive and different from zero.[17] Therefore, when rankings of firms by either value-added measure are reported, the leading firms are likely to be large firms.[18]

Table 4.9. Relationship between Size and Value-Added Measures, 1988–92

| | | Absolute Value of Economic Profit | | Absolute Value of Market Value Added | |
| | | Pearson Correlation (parametric) | Spearman Correlation (nonparametric) | Pearson Correlation (parametric) | Spearman Correlation (nonparametric) |
Year	Measure of Firm Size				
1988	Book value of equity	0.54	0.65	0.37	0.69
	Total assets	0.53	0.67	0.63	0.65
1989	Book value of equity	0.61	0.64	0.62	0.75
	Total assets	0.65	0.68	0.64	0.69
1990	Book value of equity	0.44	0.64	0.67	0.77
	Total assets	0.66	0.73	0.30	0.60
1991	Book value of equity	0.51	0.65	0.64	0.71
	Total assets	0.70	0.70	0.37	0.60
1992	Book value of equity	0.45	0.67	0.77	0.70
	Total assets	0.56	0.66	0.59	0.67

Note: All correlations are different from zero at the 5 percent level of significance.

The relation between value-added rankings and stock returns is presented in Table 4.10, where we divide each yearly sample into two categories based on whether economic profit is positive or negative. We remove those cases where the economic profit is less than 1 percent of invested capital because the possibility exists of some measurement error in our estimate of economic profit, which leads to potential misclas-

---

[16]Consider the following example. Suppose Firm A has total assets of $10 million and produces an economic value added of $1 million and Firm B has total assets of $100 million and produces an economic value added of $1 million. Which firm has the better performance? A ranking by economic value added indicates that the firms are identical in performance. In fact, however, Firm A has been able to generate the same amount of value added as Firm B but with far fewer assets. Although this issue may seem to be a trivial matter, firms have been ranked by the dollar amount of economic value added and market value added (see, for example, the rankings produced by *Fortune* in Tully [1993, 1994]).

[17]We use the absolute value of economic profit and market value added because the greater the capital to begin with, the greater the economic profit or market value added, whether positive or negative in sign. In addition, end-of-period book value of equity and total assets also correlate with economic profit and market value of equity, and the correlations are similar to those reported in Table 4.9.

[18]See, for example, the rankings by *Fortune* in Tully (1993, 1994).

Table 4.10.Stock Returns of Firms Classified by Economic Profit, 1988–92

Year	Economic Profit	Number of Firms	Average TSR	t-Statistic	Average MAR	t-Statistic	Average SAR	t-Statistic
1988	Positive	77	17.7%		−3.4%		1.0%	
	Negative	147	12.5	1.64	−4.4	0.28	−3.1	1.30
1989	Positive	73	18.1		1.9		3.1	
	Negative	131	12.0	2.01*	2.4	−0.14	1.5	0.51
1990	Positive	68	19.3		−0.2		7.4	
	Negative	153	3.4	4.43*	−8.0	2.15*	−6.0	3.83*
1991	Positive	84	16.9		−10.7		3.4	
	Negative	134	12.3	1.38	−9.6	−0.29	−4.6	2.44*
1992	Positive	111	13.0		−10.4		−6.3	
	Negative	112	20.4	−2.27*	3.5	−3.75*	4.1	−2.12*

*Indicates that the difference in mean returns between the positive and negative economic profit portfolios is different from zero at the 5 percent level of significance.

Note: Firms whose economic profit is within ±1 percent of invested capital are excluded from this analysis.

sification. Comparing the two groups for each year, we see that in four of the five years, firms with positive economic profit have greater total stock returns, on average, than firms with negative economic profit. The test of differences in mean returns for the positive and negative economic profit portfolios indicates, however, that firms with positive economic profit significantly outperformed firms with negative economic profit only in 1989 and 1990. In fact, in 1992, firms with negative economic profit performed better than firms with positive economic profit. The results using the SAR benchmark are similar to those using the TSR benchmark. The results using the MAR benchmark indicate that firms with positive economic profit outperform those with negative economic profit in one year (i.e., 1990) and underperform in another (i.e., 1992).

In Table 4.11 (1990 data), we list the top 10 firms in our sample in terms of market value added and report their respective rankings for other value-added measures and total stock returns. In this way, we can further examine how the value-added measures rank firms relative to stock returns.[19] We choose 1990 because both the economic-value-added and market-value-added measures are positively correlated with the benchmarks in that year, thus placing the value-added measures in the best light. The rankings by market value added, as shown in Panel A, do not correspond directly with the rankings by other measures, even the closely aligned economic profit measure. Although market value added and economic profit are related concepts, a direct relation exists between the two (that is, market value added equals economic profit/cost of capital) only if economic profit can be expected to be generated at that same level in perpetuity. In the top 10 market-value firms, economic profit rankings do not agree with market-value-added rankings.

In addition, market-value-added rankings do not correspond directly with stock return rankings. The top 10 firms by total stock returns for 1990 are presented in Panel B of Table 4.11.[20] Part of the explanation for this finding is that the construction of market value added, as mentioned earlier, includes the change in the book value of debt and preferred stock. Another part of the explanation is that market value added is sensitive to firm size: Adding $1 million in value is easier for large firms than for small firms. In addition, market value added (or even the percentage of market value added) does not consider the general movement of the market and the risk of the firm. A

---

[19]This table allows comparison with published rankings based on market value added.

Table 4.11. Comparison of Rankings of Sample Firms, 1990

A: Top 10 firms ranked by market value added from sample of 267 firms

Market Value Added	Company Name		Rank out of 267 Firms by:					
		TSR	Economic Profit	Return on Capital	Spread	Percentage of Change in Market Value	MARs	SARs
1	Philip Morris Companies	4	2	31	15	30	7	4
2	Merck & Company	10	3	1	1	31	28	10
3	Bristol-Myers Squibb Company	11	6	7	8	36	11	12
4	IBM Corporation	112	259	113	127	60	43	136
5	The Coca-Cola Company	16	5	2	2	44	30	23
6	PepsiCo	6	4	12	11	46	10	8
7	Johnson & Johnson	5	7	8	12	27	5	5
8	Pfizer	2	60	58	78	13	3	3
9	WMX Technologies	87	37	73	62	40	203	108
10	Exxon Corporation	33	8	79	75	66	37	43

B: Top 10 firms ranked by TSRs from sample of 267 firms

TSR	Company Name	Market Value Added	Economic Profit	Return on Capital	Spread	Percentage of Change in Market Value	MARs	SARs
1	Wendy's International	75	154	154	221	5	1	1
2	Pfizer	8	60	58	783	13	3	3
3	Southwest Airlines Company	62	185	220	222	267	2	2
4	Philip Morris	1	2	31	15	30	7	4
5	Johnson & Johnson	7	7	8	12	27	5	5
6	PepsiCo	6	4	12	11	46	10	8
7	Safety-Kleen Corporation	48	87	61	84	17	6	6
8	Service Corporation International	52	108	151	113	11	4	7
9	Kellogg Company	18	27	24	21	38	15	9
10	Merck	2	3	1	1	31	28	10

comparison of Panel B with Panel A confirms this fact: Market-value-added rankings are biased toward large firms.

Summary

Value-added measures are theoretically more closely related to firm value than the simpler, traditional measures, such as return on assets. Empirically, both traditional and value-added measures of performance are highly correlated with stock returns, with value-added measures having a slight edge over the traditional measures. The commonly used value-added measures, economic profit and market value added, which have gained much attention in the financial press, are only slightly more correlated with stock returns than the traditional measures and thus may not be better gauges of performance than traditional measures.

Enhancements to the value-added measures to reduce the effects of a size bias, such as using the return on capital or the percentage of change in market value added, improve somewhat the value-added measures and make them more attractive for performance evaluation than the traditional measures. But because we stacked the deck against the traditional measures in the empirical analysis by using the most naive form of these measures, making no adjustments in the reported accounting profit amounts and using end-of-period values for total assets and the book value of equity, it is disappointing that the more recently developed measures do not dominate the traditional measures.[21]

---

[20] In Table 4.8, we showed that a statistically significant correlation exists between the market-value-added measures and stock returns. Although that information is correct, the correlation is not perfect. For example, the correlation of 0.50 between the change in market value added and stock returns means that only 25 percent of the variation in the stock returns is explained by the market-value-added measure's variation (that is, because $R = 0.50$, $R^2 = 0.25$). Although statistically significant, this result leaves 75 percent unexplained. The imperfect correlation explains the apparent lack of relation between rankings shown in Table 4.11.

[21] One can assume that analysts make some adjustments using the traditional measures, such as placing comparable firms on the same accounting basis. The traditional measures are used in this empirical work in their simplest form.

5. Conclusions

The aim of this analysis is to see whether the value-added measures when applied to the firm as a whole align with market measures of performance. If they do, confidence is gained in using such measures to evaluate aspects of the firm's management, such as a division or a product line. In particular, those measures that do not rely on market values (which would not be available for such aspects as a division) are of particular interest. Return on capital, using the refinements in adjusting accounting data to better reflect economic reality, appears promising. This measure correlates significantly with stock price performance and does not rely on market values in its construction, but we do not find that this measure is empirically more closely related to stock returns than the traditional measures. This finding suggests that the parsimonious, but less theoretically pleasing, traditional measures should not be eliminated from consideration in performance evaluation.

From the perspective of an analyst, do value-added measures add value? The change in market value added is correlated with stock returns. Should the analyst thus use market-value-added measures to evaluate the performance of a firm? Not necessarily. Market-value-added measures may not be superior to stock returns for several reasons:

- Market-value-added measures, as strictly applied, suffer from a size bias. Even when adjustments are made to reduce this bias, market-value-added measures do not adjust for events outside the control of management, such as general market movements. On the other hand, simple adjustments can be made for market movements and security risk to improve stock returns as a measure of performance.
- Stock returns are readily available measures of firm performance that do not depend on accounting book values of capital. Stock returns can be calculated for any interval of time and do not rely on the use of accounting values, which are made available at specific intervals of time (e.g., quarterly).
- Market value added, if computed using market values of all sources of capital (not simply the market value of equity), reflects the performance of the firm in using all of its capital and is, therefore, sensitive to changes in yields. Focusing instead on the market value of equity, and hence on stock returns, does not avoid this problem completely because stock prices are also affected by market yields.

If the objective of the management of a firm is to maximize the value of equity, then stock returns, adjusted for market movements and risk, are superior to market-value-added measures in evaluating a firm's overall performance. From an analyst's perspective, market-value-added measures do not provide any information above that offered by stock returns, which is not to say that the recently developed measures of economic profit and market value added are not worthwhile. Quite the contrary. The resurgence of attention on economic profit and away from accounting profit allows managers to focus on value creation rather than on short-sighted accounting numbers.[1] This shift in focus should ultimately enhance the value of the firm.

---

[1]The calculation of economic profit for a firm, division, or product is quite detailed, however, and should be done with expertise and caution. Furthermore, the use of economic profit measures in performance evaluation should be undertaken with the understanding of the sensitivity of these measures to the methods of calculation and assumptions.

Appendix A. The Firm's Cost of Capital

The cost of capital is the rate of return that a firm must earn to satisfy its suppliers of capital—debtholders and shareholders. The term "cost of capital" is a source of confusion, however, for several reasons. First is the issue of whether what is being referred to is the firm's overall cost of capital—that is, the cost of capital for all of the firm's projects (past and present)—or the cost of capital for a specific project. The former is used in performance evaluation techniques, and the latter is used in capital budgeting applications for individual projects. In the latter case, a project's cost of capital is generally determined by first starting with the firm's overall cost of capital and then tailoring this value to reflect the project's relative riskiness.

Another source of confusion is whether what is being referred to is the marginal cost of capital or the embedded cost of capital. The marginal cost of capital is the cost of capital for raising the next dollar of capital. The marginal cost of capital is used in capital budgeting situations when evaluating whether the project's future cash flows outweigh the cost of the funds to support those cash flows. The embedded cost of capital is the cost of funds already raised—that is, what it costs the firm for the funds already supplied. In performance evaluation, an embedded rate is used because a specific period is being examined to see whether the firm created value during that period. Whether the marginal cost of capital or the embedded cost of capital is being calculated, however, the principles are the same; only the particular costs of the sources of funds are slightly different.

Cost of Debt

The cost-of-debt capital is the after-tax cost of raising additional debt. Let r_d represent the cost of debt per year before considering the tax deductibility of interest, r_d^* represent the cost of debt after considering the tax deductibility of interest, and t be the marginal tax rate. The effective cost of debt is

$$r_d^* = r_d(1 - t).$$ (A.1)

The before-tax cost of debt is estimated as the current yield on debt with similar credit risk, but a number of complications exist in estimating the current cost of debt. These complications include

*   the yield on convertible debt;
*   debt with variable interest rates that contain rate caps and floors;
*   the yield on debt denominated in a foreign currency;
*   leases for which no current yield is defined; and
*   debt that is not rated.

Cost of Preferred Stock

The cost of preferred stock is based on the valuation of a perpetuity. Let P_p indicate the present value of the preferred stock, D_p indicate the perpetual dividend per share per period, and r_p indicate the discount rate. Then,

$$P_p = \frac{D_p}{r_p}. \tag{A.2}$$

Equation A.2 can be turned around to solve for r_p, the cost of preferred stock, given P_p (the current price) and D_p:

$$r_p = \frac{D_p}{P_p}. \tag{A.3}$$

The cost of preferred stock can be proxied by, for example, discounting the current preferred dividend by the current market price of the stock or by using yields on similarly rated preferred stock.

The Cost of Common Equity

The cost of common stock is the cost of raising one more dollar of common equity capital, either internally from earnings retained in the firm or externally by issuing new shares of common stock. Costs are associated with both internally and externally generated capital. How can internally generated capital (i.e., retained earnings) have a cost? As a firm generates internal funds, some portion is used to pay off creditors and preferred shareholders. The remainder are funds owned by the common shareholders. The firm may either retain these funds (investing in assets) or pay them out to the shareholders in the form of cash dividends.

Shareholders require the firm to use retained earnings to generate a return that is at least as large as the return they could have generated for themselves if they had received as dividends the amount of funds represented in the retained earnings. Therefore, retained funds are *not* a free source of capital. The cost of internal equity funds is the opportunity cost of funds of the firm's shareholders. This opportunity cost is what shareholders could earn on these funds for the same level of risk.

The only difference between the cost of internally and externally generated funds is the cost of issuing new common stock. The cost of internally generated funds is the opportunity cost of those funds—what shareholders could have earned on those funds. But the cost of externally generated funds (that is, funds from selling new shares of stock) includes the sum of the opportunity cost and the cost of issuing the new stock (i.e., flotation costs). For now, ignore flotation costs.

The cost of issuing common stock is difficult to estimate because of the nature of the cash flow streams to common shareholders. Common shareholders receive their returns in the form of dividends and change in the price of the shares. The dividend stream is not fixed, as in the case of preferred stock. How often and how much is paid as dividends is at the discretion of the board of directors. Therefore, this stream is unknown, so determining its value is difficult. The change in the price of shares is also difficult to estimate; the price of the stock at any future point in time is influenced by investors' expectations of cash flows beyond that future point.

Nevertheless, two methods are commonly used to estimate the cost of common stock: The *dividend valuation model* (DVM) and the *capital asset pricing model* (CAPM). Each method relies on different assumptions regarding the cost of equity; each produces different estimates of the cost of common equity.

The DVM states that the price of a share of stock, P, is the present value of all its future cash dividends, where the future dividends are discounted at the required rate of return on equity, r_e:[1]

$$P = \frac{\text{Dividends in first period}}{(1 + r_e)^1} + \frac{\text{Dividends in second period}}{(1 + r_e)^2} + \dots. \quad \text{(A.4)}$$

If these dividends are constant forever, the cost of common stock (the required return on equity, r_e) is derived from the value of a perpetuity. But common stock dividends do not usually remain constant. Dividends typically grow. Let D_0 indicate this period's dividend. If dividends grow at a constant rate, g, forever, the present value of the common stock is the present value of *all* future dividends:

$$P = \frac{D_0(1 + g)^1}{(1 + r_e)^1} + \frac{D_0(1 + g)^2}{(1 + r_e)^2} + \dots + \frac{D_0(1 + g)^\infty}{(1 + r_e)^\infty}. \quad \text{(A.5)}$$

Representing the next period's dividend as $D_1 = D_0 (1 + g)$, this equation can be simplified to the familiar constant growth dividend model (or the Gordon model):[2]

$$P = D_0 \frac{1 + g}{r_e - g}$$

$$= \frac{D_1}{r_e - g}. \quad \text{(A.6)}$$

Rearranging this equation to solve for r_e produces

$$r_e = \frac{D_1}{P} + g,$$

which shows that the cost of common stock is the sum of the next period's dividend yield, D_1/P, plus the growth rate of dividends.

An alternative way to estimate the cost of equity is to take a slightly different approach to analyzing investors' required rate of return: Assuming that what investors require is compensation for both the time value of money and for risk, the CAPM can

---

[1]The DVM is attributed to Gordon (1959, 1962).

[2]Pulling today's dividend, D_0, from each term produces,

$$P = D_0 \left(\frac{(1 + g)^1}{(1 + r_e)^1} + \frac{(1 + g)^2}{(1 + r_e)^2} + \dots + \frac{(1 + g)^\infty}{(1 + r_e)^\infty} \right).$$

Expressing this equation in summation notation yields

$$P = D_0 \sum_{t=1}^{\infty} \frac{(1 + g)^t}{(1 + r_e)^t}.$$

The term $\sum_{t=1}^{\infty} \frac{(1 + g)^t}{(1 + r_e)^t}$ is approximately equal to $\frac{1 + g}{r_e - g}$.

be used to help determine the cost of common equity.

Before figuring out how much investors should be compensated for risk, the type of risk must be understood. The CAPM assumes an investor holds a diversified portfolio. The result is that the only risk left in the portfolio as a whole is the risk related to movements in the market as a whole; that is, the only relevant risk is market risk. The importance of this assumption is that because investors bear only market risk, they need only be compensated for market risk.

Assuming all shareholders hold diversified portfolios, the risk that is relevant in valuing a firm's equity is its market risk. The greater the market risk, the greater the compensation (i.e., higher yield) for bearing this risk.

In the CAPM, the cost of common stock is the sum of the investor's compensation for the time value of money and the investor's compensation for the market risk of the stock:

$$\text{Cost of common stock} = \text{Compensation for the time value of money} + \text{Compensation for market risk.} \tag{A.7}$$

The compensation for the time value of money is represented as the expected risk-free rate of interest, r_f.

If a particular common stock's market risk is *the same* as the risk of the market as a whole, then the compensation for that stock's market risk is the market risk premium. The market's risk premium is the difference between the expected return on the market, r_m, and the expected risk-free rate, r_f:

$$\text{Market risk premium} = r_m - r_f. \tag{A.8}$$

If a particular common stock has market risk that is *different* from the risk of the market as a whole, then that stock's market risk premium has to be adjusted to reflect this difference. Suppose the market risk premium is 8 percent. If a stock's market risk is twice the risk of the market as a whole, the stock's premium for its market risk is 2×8 percent, or 16 percent. If a stock's market risk is half the risk of the market as a whole, the stock's premium for market risk is 0.5×8 percent, or 4 percent. This adjustment fine-tunes the compensation investors will need to accept for that stock's market risk. The fine-tuning starts with the benchmark for the risk of the market as a whole and adjusts that risk to reflect the market's premium for the stock's relative market risk to come up with the stock's premium.

That is, with β representing the adjustment factor,

$$\text{Compensation for market risk} = \beta(r_m - r_f). \tag{A.9}$$

By knowing the compensation for the time value of money and the compensation for market risk, the cost of common stock, r_e, becomes

$$r_e = r_f + \beta (r_m - r_f). \tag{A.10}$$

The term $(r_m - r_f)$ represents the risk premium required by investors for bearing the risk of owning the market portfolio. The β multiplier fine-tunes this market risk premium to compensate for the market portfolio associated with the individual firm; β is a measure of the sensitivity of the returns on a particular security (or group of securities) to changes in the returns on the market.[3]

---

[3]A common stock with a β greater than 1.0 has more risk than the average security in the market. A common stock with a β less than 1.0 has less risk than the average security in the market.

Suppose a firm's stock has a β of 2.0. This means its market risk is twice the risk of the average security in the market. If the expected risk-free rate of interest is 6 percent and the expected return on the market is 10 percent, the cost of the firm's common stock is

$$r_e = 0.06 + [2.0(0.10 - 0.06)]$$
$$= 0.14 \text{ or } 14\%.$$

In this example, the market risk premium is 4 percent (10 percent – 6 percent). A market risk premium of 4 percent means that an investor who owns a portfolio with the same risk as the market as a whole (that is, with a β of 1.0) would expect to receive a 10 percent return composed of 6 percent to compensate for the price of time and 4 percent to compensate for the price of market risk. For a security with a β of 2.0, the investor would expect a return of 14 percent, composed of 6 percent to compensate for the price of time and 8 percent (2.0 × 4 percent) to compensate for the price of that security's particular risk.

Weighted-Average Cost of Capital

The cost of capital is the average of the cost of each source weighted by the proportion of total capital it represents. Hence, cost of capital is also referred to as the weighted-average cost of capital (WACC). Let w_d, w_p, and w_e represent the proportions of debt, preferred stock, and common stock in the capital structure, respectively, and r_d^*, r_p, and r_e equal the after-tax cost of debt, the cost of preferred stock, and the cost of common stock, respectively. The WACC then is[4]

$$\text{WACC} = w_d\, r_d^* + w_p\, r_p + w_e\, r_e. \tag{A.11}$$

Consider the following weights and marginal costs of the different sources of capital:

Source	Weight	Cost of Capital
Debt	40%	8%
Preferred stock	5	10
Common equity	55	12

The WACC for this example is

$$\text{WACC} = (0.40)(0.08) + (0.05)(0.10) + (0.55)(0.12)$$
$$= 10.1\%.$$

Issues in Calculating a WACC

Determining the cost of capital appears straightforward: Find the cost of each source of capital and weight it by the proportion it will represent in the firm's new capital. But this task is *not* so simple. Many problems arise in determining the cost of capital for an individual firm,

One such problem is forecasting the future costs of issuing debt and preferred stock. Recent offerings may help to gauge what the cost will be in the near future, but what will the cost be in the more distant future?

Another problem is the perplexing cost of equity. The DVM requires estimates of future periods' dividends. Although the model can be adjusted to allow for nonconstant dividends, this adjustment produces very rough estimates for the future. In the case of

---

[4]WACC is a *weighted average* of the different costs of capital, but each of these costs is a *marginal* cost—the cost of raising additional capital using that source. Therefore, WACC is a *marginal* cost—what it costs to raise additional capital—*averaged* across the different sources of capital.

the CAPM, what is the expected risk-free rate of interest in the future? What is the expected return on the market in the future? What is the expected sensitivity of a particular asset's return compared with that of the market's return? To answer many of these questions, estimates are derived by looking at historical data, but this approach can be hazardous.

Furthermore, complications arise with the calculation of the market value of debt for which there are variable interest rates with caps and floors and for swaps, foreign-currency-denominated debt, leases, equity-linked debt, and callable debt.

Estimating the cost of capital requires judgment and an understanding of the current risks and returns associated with the firm and its securities as well as an understanding of the firm's and its securities' future risks and returns.

Appendix B. Net Present Value and Internal Rate of Return

The net present value (NPV) is the present value of a project's cash flows. These cash flows include both the inflows and the outflows; the primary outflows involve the investment outlay at the beginning of the project's life; the inflows are expected periodically during the project's life. The discount rate used to translate the cash flows to the present is the investment's cost of capital. The cost of capital is the rate of return that suppliers of capital (debt and equity) require for the project. This required rate reflects the riskiness of the project; the riskier the project, the higher the project's cost of capital.

NPV can be represented using summation notation, where t indicates any particular period, CF_t represents the expected cash flow at the end of period t, r represents the project's cost of capital, and T represents the number of periods composing the economic life of the investment:[1]

$$NPV = \sum_{t=1}^{T} \frac{CF_t}{(1+r)^t} - I, \tag{B.1}$$

where I is the investment made in Period 0 (the initial period). For any future period t, all estimated cash flows (positive and negative) are collected and netted together. Cash inflows are positive values of CF_t, and cash outflows are negative values of CF_t.

The NPV is the dollar value change in the value of the firm that is expected to result from the investment in the project. A positive NPV indicates that the investment creates value; a negative NPV indicates that the investment is value destroying.

The internal rate of return (IRR) is a related measure. The calculation of IRR involves solving for IRR in the equation:

$$0 = \sum_{t=1}^{T} \frac{CF_t}{(1+IRR)^t} - I. \tag{B.2}$$

Decision making using IRR requires comparing the IRR with the cost of capital for the investment: If the IRR exceeds the cost of capital, the investment is value enhancing; if the IRR is less than the cost of capital, the investment is value destroying. The investment's cost of capital, therefore, becomes a hurdle. Another way to view the IRR is that it is the discount rate that causes the net present value to be equal to zero.

In most cases, the NPV and IRR measures produce the same decision regarding a

---

[1]We use the notation r to represent the firm's cost of capital for the investment project, which is the marginal cost of one dollar of additional capital for this project. The weighted-average cost of capital, as calculated in Appendix A, is a method of estimating r for the firm as a whole. In practice, WACC is used as a starting point for estimating r for a given project. For example, if the project is a new product that is riskier than the firm's typical project, an estimate of r may be WACC plus, say, 5 percent.

project's profitability, although several exceptions are discussed in detail in most introductory finance texts. In those cases where the NPV and IRR disagree, the NPV is the preferred measure.[2]

---

[2]A source of conflict exists between the NPV and the IRR in making decisions because of the different reinvestment assumptions of the two methods. The NPV mathematics assume that all intermediate cash flows are reinvested in projects that yield the cost of capital. The IRR mathematics assume that all intermediate cash flows are reinvested in projects that yield the IRR. The latter is generally a more aggressive assumption to make in actual capital budgeting situations.

Glossary

Basic earning power ratio: The ratio of the earnings from operations (earnings before interest and taxes) to total assets; a measure of the effectiveness of operations.

Capital: The net investment in a firm by the suppliers of capital; the net assets of the firm calculated as the difference between the total assets of the firm and the current, non-interest-bearing liabilities.

Cash flow return on investment (CFROI): The return on a firm's investment calculated using estimated inflation-adjusted gross investment, inflation-adjusted gross cash flow, and inflation-adjusted nondepreciable assets.

Comparative advantage: An advantage that one firm has over another in the cost of producing or distributing goods or services.

Competitive advantage: An advantage that one firm has over another because of the structure of the markets in which they operate.

Cost of capital: The marginal cost of an additional dollar of capital; the weighted average of the costs of the capital expected to be raised by the firm to support future investment opportunities.

Economic profit: The difference between revenues and costs over a period of time, where costs comprise expenditures, opportunity costs, and normal profits.

Economic value added. The dollar amount of value added over a specified period of time. Also known as economic profit.

Franchise P/E: The amount by which the P/E of a firm exceeds the base P/E, which is the P/E considering growth at the market discount rate.

Franchise value: The value of a firm attributed to future investment opportunities that are expected to produce a return in excess of the market return.

Free cash flow: The cash flow of a firm less any capital expenditures.

Internal rate of return (IRR): The discount rate that equates the present value of an investment's future cash flows to the investment's cost; the rate of return on an investment, assuming that all intermediate cash flows are invested in projects with an identical rate of return.

Market value added: The increase in the firm's value over a period, controlling for the capital used to generate the change in value; the difference between the market value of the firm and the value of the firm's capital.

Net present value (NPV): The present value of future cash flows of an investment project less the present value of the investment's cash flows discounted at the cost of capital; a measure of the enhancement of shareholders' wealth arising from investment decisions.

Normal profit: The minimum return of a firm necessary for the suppliers of capital to retain their investment in the firm.

Operating capital: Capital less goodwill and any excess cash and marketable securities.

P/E: The ratio of the price per share of stock to the earnings per share of stock; often used as a proxy for future growth potential.

Return on assets: The ratio of net income to total assets; ROA provides a measure of how profitably and efficiently a firm is using its assets.

Return on capital: The ratio of net operating profit after taxes to capital.

Return on equity: The ratio of net income to the book value of equity; ROE provides a measure of the return to shareholders' investment in the firm.

Return on investment: The ratio of the benefit from an investment to the resources used; ROI ratios include the basic earning power ratio, the return on assets, and the return on equity.

Tobin's *q*: The ratio of the market value of a firm's assets to the replacement cost of the firm's assets; it is interpreted as a measure of performance because it captures the value of the firm's intangibles.

Weighted-average cost of capital (WACC): The arithmetic average of the costs of the firm's capital from different sources (i.e., debt, preferred stock, and common stock), where the cost of each source is weighted by the proportion the source represents in the firm's target capital structure.

References

American Management Association. 1960. "Executive Committee Control Charts." *AMA Management Bulletin*, no. 6:22.

Birchard, B. 1994. "Mastering the New Metrics." *CFO*, vol. 10, no. 10 (October):30–38.

Brigham, E.F. 1995. *Fundamentals of Financial Management*, 7th ed. Fort Worth, TX: The Dryden Press.

Brossy, R., and J.E. Balkcom. 1994. "Getting Executives to Create Value." *Journal of Business Strategy*, vol. 15, no. 1 (January–February):18–21.

Byrne, J.A., and L. Bongiorno. 1995. "CEO Pay: Ready for Takeoff." *Business Week*, no. 3421 (April 24):88–119.

Chan, L.K., Y. Hamao, and J. Lakonishok. 1990. "Fundamentals and Stock Returns in Japan." *Journal of Finance*, vol. 46, no. 5 (December):1739–64.

Chung, K.H., and S.W. Pruitt. 1994. "A Simple Approximation of Tobin's *q*." *Financial Management*, vol. 23, no. 3 (Autumn):70–74.

Copeland, T., T. Koller, and J. Murrin. 1994. *Valuation: Measuring and Managing the Value of Companies*, 2nd ed. New York: John Wiley & Sons.

Fama, E.F., and K.R. French. 1992. "The Cross-Section of Expected Stock Returns." *Journal of Finance*, vol. 47, no. 2 (June):427–65.

———. 1995. "Size and Book-to-Market Factors in Earnings and Returns." *Journal of Finance*, vol. 50, no. 1 (March):131–55.

Gordon, M. 1959. "Dividends, Earnings and Stock Prices." *Review of Economics and Statistics*, vol. 41, no. 2 (May):99–105.

———. 1962. *The Investment Financing and Valuation of the Corporation*. Homewood, IL: R.D. Irwin.

Hagin, R.L. 1988. "Engineered Investment Strategies: Problems and Solutions." In *Equity Markets and Valuation Methods*. Edited by Katrina F. Sherrerd. Charlottesville, VA: Institute of Chartered Financial Analysts.

Harris, R.S., and F.C. Marston. 1994. "Value versus Growth Stocks: Book-to-Market, Growth, and Beta." *Financial Analysts Journal*, vol. 50, no. 5 (September/October):18–24.

Haugen, R.A. 1995. *The New Finance: The Case Against Efficient Markets*. Englewood Cliffs, NJ: Prentice-Hall.

Healy, P. 1985. "The Effect of Bonus Schemes on Accounting Decisions." *Journal of Accounting & Economics*, vol. 7, nos. 1–3 (April):85–113.

Holthausen, R.W., D.F. Larcker, and R.G. Sloan. 1995. "Annual Bonus Schemes and the Manipulation of Earnings." *Journal of Accounting & Economics*, vol. 19, no. 1 (February):29–74.

Jones, T.P. 1995. "The Economic Value-Added Approach to Corporate Investment." In *Corporate Financial Decision Making and Equity Analysis*. Edited by Randall S. Billingsley. Charlottesville, VA: AIMR.

Kogelman, S., and M.L. Leibowitz. 1995. "The Franchise Factor Valuation Approach: Capturing the Firm's Investment Opportunities." In *Corporate Financial Decision Making and Equity Analysis*. Edited by Randall S. Billingsley. Charlottesville, VA: AIMR.

Lakonishok, J., A. Shleifer, and R.W. Vishny. 1994. "Contrarian Investment, Extrapolation, and Risk." *Journal of Finance*, vol. 49, no. 5 (December):11541–1578.

Leibowitz, M.L., and S. Kogelman. 1990. "Inside the P/E Ratio: The Franchise Factor." *Financial Analysts Journal*, vol. 46, no. 6 (November/December):17–35.

Leibowitz, M.L., and S. Kogelman. 1994. *Franchise Value and the Price/Earnings Ratio*. Charlottesville, VA: The Research Foundation of the Institute of Chartered Financial Analysts.

Lindenberg, E.B., and S.A. Ross. 1981. "Tobin's *q* Ratio and Industrial Organization." *Journal of Business*, vol. 54, no. 1 (January):1–32.

Madden, B.J. 1995. "The Case for Cash Flow ROI in Linking Company Performance with Market Valuation." *Valuation Issues*, vol. 1, no. 3 (November):4–7.

Marshall, A. 1890. *Principles of Economics.* New York: Macmillan, vol. 1:142.

Myers, S. 1984. "Finance Theory and Financial Strategy." *Interfaces*, vol. 14, no. 1 (January–February):126–37.

Perfect, S.B., and K.W. Wiles. 1994. "Alternative Construction of Tobin's *q*: An Empirical Comparison." *Journal of Empirical Finance*, vol. 1, no. 3/4 (July):313–41.

Peterson, P. 1994. *Financial Management and Analysis.* New York: McGraw-Hill.

Reimann, B.C. 1988. "Decision Support Software for Value-Based Planning." *Planning Review*, vol. 16, no. 2 (March/April):22–32.

Rosenberg, B., K. Reid, and R. Lanstein. 1985. "Persuasive Evidence of Market Inefficiency." *Journal of Portfolio Management*, vol. 11, no. 3 (Spring):9–16.

Ross, S. 1994. "Survivorship Bias in Performance Studies." In *Blending Quantitative and Traditional Equity Analysis.* Edited by H. Russell Fogler. Charlottesville, VA: AIMR.

Rutledge, J. 1993. "De-jargoning EVA." *Forbes,* vol. 152, no. 10 (October 25):148.

Saint, D.K. 1995. "Why Economic Value Is a Yardstick for Numbers, Not People." *Financial Executive*, vol. 11, no. 2 (March/April):9–11.

Sheehan, T.J. 1994. "To EVA or Not to EVA: Is That the Question?" *Journal of Applied Corporate Finance*, vol. 7, no. 2 (Summer):84–87.

Stern, J. 1993a. "Value and People Management," *Corporate Finance*, no. 104 (July 1993):35–37.

———.1993b. "EVA: Share Options that Maximize Value." *Corporate Finance*, no. 105 (August):31–32.

———. 1994. "No Incentive for Bad Management." *Corporate Finance* (March):43–44.

"Stern Stewart EVA Roundtable." 1994. *Journal of Applied Corporate Finance*, vol. 7, no. 2 (Summer):46–70.

Stewart, G.B. III. 1991. *The Quest for Value.* New York: Harper Collins.

———. 1994. "EVA: Fact and Fantasy." *Journal of Applied Corporate Finance*, vol. 7, no. 2 (Summer):71–84.

Thomas, R., and L. Edwards. 1993. "For Good Decisions, Determine Business Values More Accurately." *Corporate CashFlow*, vol. 14, no. 9 (September):37–40.

Tobin, J. 1969. "A General Equilibrium Approach to Monetary Theory." *Journal of Money, Credit, and Banking*, vol. 1, no. 1 (February):15–29.

Tully, S. 1993. "The Real Key to Creating Wealth." *Fortune*, vol. 128, no. 6 (September 20):38–50.

———. 1994. "America's Best Wealth Creators." *Fortune*, vol. 130, no. 11 (November 28):143–62.

Walbert, L. 1993. "America's Best Wealth Creators." *Fortune*, vol. 128, no. 16 (December 27):64–76.

Selected AIMR Publications

AIMR Performance Presentation Standards Handbook, 2nd edition, 1996

The Consumer Staples Industry, 1996

Global Equity Investing, 1996

Global Portfolio Management, 1996
Jan R. Squires, CFA, *Editor*

Investing Worldwide VII: Focus on Emerging Markets, 1996

Managing Endowment and Foundation Funds, 1996

Managing Investment Firms: People and Culture, 1996
Jan R. Squires, CFA, *Editor*

The Media Industry, 1996

Merck & Company: A Comprehensive Equity Valuation Analysis, 1996
Randall S. Billingsley, CFA

Risk Management, 1996

Standards of Practice Casebook, 1996

Standards of Practice Handbook, 7th edition, 1996

A full catalog of publications is available on AIMR's World Wide Web site at **www.aimr.org**; or you may write to AIMR, P.O. Box 3668, Charlottesville, VA 22903 U.S.A.; call 1-804-980-3668; fax 1-804-980-9755; or e-mail **info@aimr.org** to receive a free copy. All prices are subject to change.